T0305589

REGENERATIVE BUSINESS VOICES

This is a book about the future of sustainability. *Regenerative Business Voices: Values-based Entrepreneurship for Sustainable Enterprises* tells the stories of four regenerative organizations and the people who founded them and guided them towards sustaining futures.

Regenerative sustainability recognizes the urgency of transforming organizations to reverse the unsustainable pathways we are currently on. Regenerative businesses do not simply do less harm, or produce zero emissions, or optimize the efficient use of natural resources; they also restore and enhance well-being in social and ecological systems. The stories presented here are analyzed using the business ethics approach called Giving Voice to Values (GVV). Through the application of GVV principles, we uncover the processes involved in how regenerative businesses develop and function, and gain insights into how business leaders voice their deep convictions, overcome silencing rationalizations, normalize their execution of personal choice, discover deep purpose in their work, and draw on their personal histories to create new ways of doing business. We present and analyze these cases to understand how and why expressing values can be so crucial in developing sustainable businesses, and to provide practical examples of how individuals can generate enthusiasm, counter objections, gain allies, and prepare for and practice conversations that help them move forward.

The book offers managers and sustainability consultants a new way of understanding some of the central dynamics involved in business ethics and organizational change for sustainability. We hope the book will be immensely valuable to educators, business students, and practitioners interested in sustainability, environmental business ethics, and corporate social responsibility topics.

Mark G. Edwards was Associate Professor at Jönköping International Business School (JIBS) from 2017–2023. He is now an affiliated teacher with JIBS's Media, Management and Transformation Centre and with the Business School, University of Western Australia.

Anton Lindberg is a sustainability consultant and works at Hållbarhetsteamet i Sverige AB, Sweden. As a freelancer, he has also worked with various sustainability projects internationally.

Melker Larsson is a business entrepreneur and sustainability consultant with Hållbarhetsteamet i Sverige AB, Sweden. He co-founded, produces, and hosts *The Decade*, a podcast on regenerative sustainability. He is CEO of ATOBE, hosting eco-friendly outdoor endurance events.

Jonathan Angel is a sustainability consultant at Hållbarhetsteamet i Sverige AB, in Sweden. He co-founded and hosts *The Decade* podcast. He is also a professional sports coach focusing on mental training.

Giving Voice to Values
Series Editors: Jerry Goodstein, Brian Moriarty and Daniel Arce

The *Giving Voice to Values* series is a collection of books on Business Ethics and Corporate Social Responsibility that brings a practical, solutions-oriented, skill-building approach to the salient questions of values-driven leadership.

Giving Voice to Values (GVV: www.GivingVoiceToValues.org) – the curriculum, the pedagogy and the research upon which it is based – was designed to transform the foundational assumptions upon which the teaching of business ethics is based, and importantly, to equip future business leaders to know not only what is right – but how to make it happen.

Tactics for Racial Justice
Building an Antiracist Organization and Community
Shannon Joyce Prince

The Lawyer's Guide to Business Ethics
Keith William Diener

Authentic Excellence for Organizations
Creating Flourishing "&" Cultures
R. Kelly Crace, Charles J. Hardy and Robert L. Crace

Giving Voice to Values-based Leadership
How to Develop Good Organizations through Work on Values
Gry Espedal and Frank Elter

Socratic Dialogue
Voicing Values
Sira Abenoza and Josep M. Lozano

Regenerative Business Voices
Values-based Entrepreneurship for Sustainable Enterprises
Mark G. Edwards, Anton Lindberg, Melker Larsson, and Jonathan Angel

For more information about this series, please visit: www.routledge.com/ Giving-Voice-to-Values/book-series/GVV

REGENERATIVE BUSINESS VOICES

Values-based Entrepreneurship for Sustainable Enterprises

Mark G. Edwards, Anton Lindberg, Melker Larsson, and Jonathan Angel

Routledge
Taylor & Francis Group

LONDON AND NEW YORK

Designed cover image: Getty Images

First published 2024
by Routledge
4 Park Square, Milton Park, Abingdon, Oxon OX14 4RN

and by Routledge
605 Third Avenue, New York, NY 10158

Routledge is an imprint of the Taylor & Francis Group, an informa business

© 2024 Mark G. Edwards, Anton Lindberg, Melker Larsson, and Jonathan Angel

British Library Cataloguing-in-Publication Data
A catalogue record for this book is available from the British Library

Library of Congress Cataloging-in-Publication Data
Names: Edwards, Mark G., author. | Lindberg, Anton, author. | Larsson, Melker, author. | Angel, Jonathan, author.
Title: Regenerative business voices: values-based entrepreneurship for sustainable enterprises / Mark G. Edwards, Anton Lindberg, Melker Larsson and Jonathan Angel.
Description: Abingdon, Oxon; New York, NY: Routledge, 2024. | Series: Giving voice to values, 2578-5060 | Includes bibliographical references and index.
Identifiers: LCCN 2023049443 (print) | LCCN 2023049444 (ebook) | ISBN 9781032345727 (hardback) | ISBN 9781032343273 (paperback) | ISBN 9781003330660 (ebook)
Subjects: LCSH: Sustainable development. | Environmental policy. | Social change--Environmental aspects. | Human ecology. | Social evolution.
Classification: LCC HC79.E5 E329 2024 (print) | LCC HC79.E5 (ebook) | DDC 338.9/27--dc23/eng/20231107
LC record available at https://lccn.loc.gov/2023049443
LC ebook record available at https://lccn.loc.gov/2023049444

ISBN: 978-1-032-34572-7 (hbk)
ISBN: 978-1-032-34327-3 (pbk)
ISBN: 978-1-003-33066-0 (ebk)

DOI: 10.4324/9781003330660

Typeset in Joanna MT Std
by SPi Technologies India Pvt Ltd (Straive)

CONTENTS

About the authors   viii
Acknowledgments   x

1   Core values for a regenerative world   1

2   Giving voice to regenerative values   27

3   Values and choice in Earth Regeneration   53

4   Commonland and normalizing the new   85

5   The most precious metal on Earth   112

6   The natural wealth of seaweed   139

7   Giving voice to a regenerative future   169

    Glossary   193
    Index   199

AUTHORS

Mark G. Edwards

Affiliation: Jonkoping International Business School, Media, Management and Transformation Centre, Sweden

Mark was Associate Professor in Business Administration and worked at Jönköping International Business School (JIBS) from 2017–2023. He is currently teaching at the Business School, University of Western Australia. His teaching has focused on sustainable business development, business ethics, big picture approaches to social science, and global sustainability transitions. Current research interests include sustainability and growth, news media coverage of Covid-19 and sustainability, and regenerative business practices. Mark has published his research with Routledge and Cambridge University Press and in a wide variety of scientific journals, including *Academy of Management Learning and Education, Business Strategy and the Environment*, the *Journal of Business Ethics*, and *Business & Society*.

Anton Lindberg

Affiliation: Hållbarhetsteamet i Sverige AB, Sweden

Anton holds a bachelor's degree in Sustainable Enterprise Development from Jönköping International Business School. At the time of co-authoring this book, he is working as a sustainability consultant for the consultancy firm Hållbarhetsteamet i Sverige AB, where he seeks to foster the transformation of organizations and businesses in Sweden and abroad. Anton has decided to dedicate his professional career to the purpose of restoring and regenerating socio-ecological systems through his work with organizations and businesses. For Anton, writing this book has been a new and exciting way of contributing to these efforts.

Melker Larsson

Affiliation: Hållbarhetsteamet i Sverige AB, The Decade AB, ATOBE AB, Sweden

Melker holds a BA in Sustainable Enterprise Development and is a sustainability consultant at Hållbarhetsteamet i Sverige AB in Jönköping in Sweden. He is also co-founder, producer, and host for the podcast *The Decade AB*, which is "a holistic learning journey about sustainability and regeneration". Melker is CEO and Race Director at ATOBE AB, a business that creates memorable experiences for our swim-run competitors. Melker's work mission is to help to co-create a future where humans and nature thrive. His work revolves around consulting businesses, creating inspirational content and meaningful experiences for people in nature. He aims to help people and society live lives based on awe rather than fear.

Jonathan Angel

Affiliation: Hållbarhetsteamet i Sverige AB, The Decade AB, Sweden

Jonathan holds a BA in Sustainable Enterprise Development and is a sustainability consultant at Hållbarhetsteamet i Sverige AB in Jönköping in Sweden. He is also co-founder, producer, and host for the podcast *The Decade AB*, which is "a holistic learning journey about sustainability and regeneration". Jonathan has a background in professional sport and is currently the coach of Habo Wolley, one of the top volleyball clubs in Sweden. Jonathan is a positive and driven life enthusiast who aims to be guided by love, curiosity, and compassion. He is constantly on a mission to grow and develop into the best version of himself while having his feelers out for possibilities to co-create a better future for all species and the planet.

ACKNOWLEDGMENTS

This book was partly funded by the collaborative project Social Innovation för Regional Utveckling (SIRU 2.0). SIRU 2.0 is a collaboration between the Swedish agencies Coompanion, Region Jönköpings län, and Jönköping International Business School and is financed by the European Regional Development Fund and Region Jönköpings län.

EUROPEAN UNION
European Regional Development Fund

1

CORE VALUES FOR A REGENERATIVE WORLD

Humanity is facing a global crossroad – to continue with Business-As-Usual and risk the consequences of a destabilized world or to take up the challenge of transitioning to a more sustainable and equitable one. With this introduction we provide a background to this dilemma and to the ethics and values that underpin it. This challenge also presents an opportunity for regenerative sustainability, and we describe and discuss this important new vision for deep forms of sustainable organization. We introduce the reader to the Earth System science of the Anthropocene, present a summary of the book chapters, and give pointers for how the book can be used to explore the world of regenerative businesses and the entrepreneurs that develop and energize them.

DOI: 10.4324/9781003330660-1

A regenerative world

In his opening statements to the United Nations Climate Change Conference of the Parties in Sharm El Sheikh, Egypt (COP27), the UN Secretary General António Guterres said:

> We are on a highway to climate hell with our foot still on the accelerator ... One thing is certain: those that give up are sure to lose. So, let's fight together – and let's win, for the eight billion members of our human family – and for generations to come.
> (UN Secretary General António Guterres, opening COP27, Nov 2022)

Guterres paints a gloomy picture in the first part of this quote, but he does so because he is aware of the science that underpins the likelihood of worsening impacts of climate change. The second part of the quote is more hopeful, and he asks us to work together for humanity's future. In the following pages we explore how some business entrepreneurs are also aware of the challenges but are setting to work to change business, to reframe the purpose of organizational life, and to take the collective foot of economics and business off the fossil fuel accelerator "to climate hell". We delve into how these creative and visionary leaders are building regenerative organizations through voicing their core values. We find out what these pathfinders are doing to enact their values in the creation of new forms of sustainable business.

The urgent need for ambitious organizations that take up the challenge of meeting sustainability imperatives grows with each passing year. Many are frustrated by the lack of global progress in addressing the grand environmental challenges we face. The opening quote here from Secretary General Guterres is the clear-sighted view of a concerned world leader who understands the basic climate science and its implications for the global community. Tackling climate change, and the rest of the panoply of environmental and social challenges facing economies, requires of humanity two basic responses. The first is to appreciate the urgency of what science is telling us (the first part of the Guterres quote). The second is to creatively explore the transformative opportunities that these crises present (the second part of the quote). Winston Churchill said, "Never let a good crisis go to waste". Crisis and opportunity go hand in hand. In this book we explore four remarkable cases of organizations that are not letting the global sustainability crisis "go to waste". We find out what the founders and leaders of these businesses and community enterprises are doing to turn 'Spaceship Earth' around to a new direction. These entrepreneurs share Guterres' sense of urgency, and, more importantly, their organizations are creating new pathways to regenerative futures.

The latest Earth system science tells us that the global economy needs to be well down the road to decarbonization by the end of this decade, if massive social and ecological shocks from climate change are to be avoided (IPCC et al., 2022). In recent years, regenerativity has emerged as an ambitious form of organizing and doing business that takes on board the science and creatively responds to these grand planetary challenges. Regenerativity aims to address both the social and the environmental sides of these problems in transformative ways. Because private and public organizations are the major players in causing these global changes, economic transformation will not occur without significant shifts in the ways they operate. That action will not take place without corresponding growth in organizational and entre-preneurial ethics. In this book we explore the connections between eth-ics, action, and regenerative business. We take Mary Gentile's respected and widely applied business ethics pedagogy of Giving Voice to Values (GVV) to be our guide in disclosing the details of how regenerative entrepreneurs voice their values through their organizational innovations. GVV, through its core pillars of values, voice, purpose, choice, normalization, self-story, and rationalizations, is eminently suited to uncovering the micro-foundational processes involved in how regenerative entrepreneurs operate.

Regenerative Business Voices: Values-Based Entrepreneurship for Sustainable Enterprises describes how ordinary businesspeople and community leaders have trans-formed their work and their workplaces through enacting their dreams of possibility. Here are stories in which businesspeople changed their work and the working lives of those around them through voicing their values. We apply the GVV approach to describe and analyze four organizational stories of regenerativity. These cases provide insights into how people have expressed their hopes and concerns and changed the way they do busi-ness and shifted the conversation towards more sustainable forms of oper-ating. These are positive stories, but they are also stories of how people expressed their core values in difficult circumstances and against signif-icant barriers. Each of the case-based chapters explore why, how, when, and where business leaders creatively express their values. The case analyses provide practical examples and guidance on how individuals can generate innovation and enthusiasm, how they overcome obstacles, build allies and networks of support, and how they express their values to move towards achieving their core purposes.

In the next chapter we will have more to say about GVV and how it will be applied in the following chapters. However, it is important to note from the beginning that GVV does not take a conventional perspective of business ethics or how ethical cultures can be developed. Although GVV recognizes the role of such things, the reader will find very little mention of rules, codes, or discussion of legal compliance in the following pages. In adopting the GVV approach we emphasize the connections between innovation, moral imagination, finding one's voice, and performative action. The concept of performativity is an important one for action-based theories of ethics. Performativity is not seen here as a superficial act of hypocrisy designed to give the appearance of commitment. On the contrary, performativity as we use it here refers to the social power of discourse and activity to create possibilities. Performativity is the power of language and conversation to effect change. Language does not only describe the world but acts as a creative social force to shape it. The theory of performative action (Austin, 1975; Butler, 1997; Plotnikof & Mumby, 2023) posits that "everyday discourse and communicative practices—talk, interactions, texts, visuals, symbols—co-constitute organizing" (Plotnikof & Mumby, 2023, p. 2). In other words, performativity is the act of engaging in social interactions which mediate learning and the performance of some new skill. Drawing on the ideas of Butler (1997), performative-oriented design can be thought of as the recursive power of discourse, social exchange, and communication to produce new behavioral abilities that, in turn, intentionally guide learning and the display of knowledge.

From a performative perspective, ethics is as much about creating something new through experimental action as much as it is about applying tried-and-tested moral principles. One thing that might strike the reader about the stories that follow is the positive delight that the entrepreneurs experience in creating their organizational initiatives. We will come back to this theme of ethics, positivity, and responding to grand organizational challenges several times throughout the book. We hope that the stories not only inspire students, academics, and practitioners but also provide some practical direction for how they might express and enact their own core values in realizing sustainable futures. In the rest of this introduction, we look in more detail at the topic of urgency and at the question why are entrepreneurs and leaders taking the risk of building organizations with new kinds of regenerative purposes and novel approaches to doing sustainability. To answer this, we start with the science and the latest knowledge we have about the current state of health of the planet.

The Anthropocene, global pandemics, and business

Over the past 30 years of Earth system science research a clear pattern has emerged in the underlying causes of the global environmental crisis. The burning of fossil fuels is driving climate change, the devastation of functional and genetic biodiversity is causing pandemics and species loss, the overuse of fertilizers is eutrophying rivers and coastal waterways, the mass manufacturing of novel materials such as plastics is polluting the oceans, and land use change through the industrialization of farming practices is driving desertification and soil loss. The pattern behind all these phenomena is that accelerating levels of human economic activity are driving massive levels of biophysical degradation across the planet. Humanity now moves more soil than all natural forces, fixes more nitrogen from the air than all plants, has manufactured more stuff by weight than all biomass on the planet (Elhacham, Ben-Uri, Grozovski, Bar-On, & Milo, 2020; Gaffney & Steffen, 2017). We have changed the composition and physical properties of the atmosphere and the oceans (Li, England, Hogg, Rintoul, & Morrison, 2023) and have been responsible for a decline in animal populations of almost 70% in the last 50 years (Almond, Grooten, Juffe Bignoli, & Petersen, 2022). The numbers of animals have dropped to the point where leading biologists fear we are triggering the 'Sixth Mass Extinction' event (Barnosky et al., 2011; Cowie, Bouchet, & Fontaine, 2022; Spalding & Hull, 2021). Climate change feeds into this disturbing picture with its own set of daunting facts and complex challenges. At the Conference of Parties meeting for 2022 (COP27), one of the most concerning presentations was from the eminent natural scientist Johan Rockström. Rockström said that:

> We need to have more frequent catastrophic risk assessment analyses ... because we are so close to tipping points, so close to hitting the limits of adaptation.

This era of human-induced change, called the Anthropocene, the human epoch, is characterized by the scale and pace of the loss in stability and resilience of the Earth's ecological systems.

The current Anthropocene epoch (only seven decades old) was immediately preceded by the Holocene. The Holocene was a geological period lasting almost 11,000 years and characterized by relative stability in surface temperature, sea levels, trade winds, and rainfall. This stability in climate and environmental conditions enabled the development of cities, agriculture, and many of the basic features of modern economies. The storing of surpluses, the building up of capital, the expansion of international land and sea trading, the specialization of labor, rudimentary forms of economic planning, and the development of monetary forms of exchange were all made possible through the predictability of stable agricultural seasons and climactic conditions. But the recent emergence of the Anthropocene has changed all that. As the Covid-19 pandemic amply illustrates, the VUCA world of Volatility, Uncertainty, Complexity/Chaos, and Ambiguity now dominates (Worley & Jules, 2020). The Anthropocene era is thought to have started with the advent of industrialization in the 18th century. However, it was only in the second half of the 20th century that the Anthropocene began to significantly impact on the stability of global biophysical systems. This period of exponential economic growth, called the "Great Acceleration" (Steffen, Broadgate, Deutsch, Gaffney, & Ludwig, 2015), brought with it the unprecedented levels of economic wealth but also resulted in massive and ever-increasing degradation of the natural systems that were the material source of that wealth.

Over the past 70 years the power and dynamism of market-based capitalism, technological innovation, and world trade has brought immense wealth and opportunity to some and higher living standards to many, but it has also come at staggering environmental cost. The impact of biophysical damage means that the natural replenishment and resilience of Earth's natural systems has been severely undercut. Societies across the planet are caught in a collision between unsustainable systems of economic production-consumption and rapidly diminishing ecological systems on which all economic activity depends. The cascading crises we are surrounded by today are caused by this global gridlock of economic wealth, opportunity, aspiration, poverty, pollution, climate disruption, and ecological collapse.

All the elements of this gridlock are interconnected. Economies and societies are intimately connected with natural ecologies and biophysical processes, so much so that we might better think of them as *social-ecological systems* that are tightly coupled rather than separated. An illustration of this can be seen in the origins of Covid-19 and other 21st-century pandemics. Covid-19 was caused by zoonotic spillover, that is, the transmission of pathogens from animals to humans. That spillover occurs due to ongoing disruption and destruction of the ecological systems that make this planet habitable (Garry, 2022; Gibb et al., 2020; Keesing & Ostfeld, 2021; Pekar et al., 2022; Plowright et al., 2021; Worobey et al., 2022a, 2022b). The causal connections between global phenomena like climate change and disease pandemics, as well as social crises such as population displacement and civil conflict or media ownership and climate inaction, are striking and hold important implications for how we collectively pursue our human interests. These kinds of global developments call for a restoration of the integrity and viability of the social-ecological systems of the planet. This will not happen without deep transformative shifts in how we do business. But transformation is difficult and cannot be undertaken without marked shifts in both the fundamental assumptions and basic practices that business is based on.

The sad history of climate change science and policy development sheds light on just how difficult economic transformations can be. Thirty years of reports from the Intergovernmental Panel on Climate Change (IPCC) have warned us ever more stridently about the dangers of Business-As-Usual (BAU) systems of economic consumption and production. But the response from governments and business has had no impact on the scale and rate of Green House Gas (GHG) emissions at the global level (IPCC et al., 2022). In his response to the latest IPCC Assessment Reports (AR6) released in 2022 the Secretary General of the United Nations, António Guterres, said:

> The jury has reached a verdict. And it is damning. This report of the Intergovernmental Panel on Climate Change is a litany of broken climate promises. It is a file of shame, cataloguing the empty pledges that put us firmly on track towards an unlivable world. We are on a fast track to climate disaster. ... Some Government and business leaders are saying one thing but doing another. Simply put, they are lying. And the results will be catastrophic. This is a climate emergency. Climate scientists warn that we are already perilously close to tipping points

> that could lead to cascading and irreversible climate impacts. But, high-emitting Governments and corporations are not just turning a blind eye, they are adding fuel to the flames.
>
> (United Nations, 2022)

It is not only the challenge of the "climate emergency" that confronts us. Comparable stories can be told of functional[1] and genetic[2] biodiversity loss, deforestation, zoonotic disease outbreaks, ocean pollution, eutrophication of waterways, land system change, and the associated disenfranchisement of indigenous and traditional communities. The implications of this are clear at the global level but extraordinarily difficult to act on at more local scales of engagement. To restore the global resilience and generativity of the climate and of ecological systems, the international economic system and the forms of business and commerce that constitute it need to be radically transformed. It is not just GHG emissions that need to be addressed but the whole pattern of commercial interactions that occur between business, society, and nature. But how to do this at the level of local businesses that need to compete, make money, meet government regulations, and satisfy customers? From a business ethics perspective, how do we aspire to and act on new moral commitments while surrounded by the status quo of operating businesses that reward BAU values, by outdated regulations, by isolating technologies and automated systems of big data analysis, and by market practices that inhibit the expression of values that challenge conventional priorities?

In this book we describe businesses that tackle these questions. We explore how some businesspeople are reimagining the purpose and impact of business. Sustainability-oriented entrepreneurs are developing new kinds of organizations and novel approaches to running a business that situate human commercial activities firmly within a social-ecological reality. They are moving away from the BAU focus on profits, return on investment (ROI), and financial Key Performance Indicators (KPIs) to seek out instead Key Values Indicators (KVIs), inspirational returns and the opportunities that accompany a deep sense of responsibility for the real social-ecological impacts of business. Rather than exiting the domain of business or silencing their concerns, they work to express their values through harnessing the energy and impact of business as a restorative and regenerative agent in the world. In the following pages we explore how and why they are voicing their values to forge a way forward into this new way of imagining and operating in the world of commerce, real value creation and radical sustainability.

Beyond 'net zero'

There is much debate in the development of climate change policies about 'zero emissions', 'mission zero', and 'targeting net zero'. All this refers, of course, to the urgent need to minimize net increase in GHG emissions to hold the increase of global surface temperatures to between 1.5° and 2.0° Celsius. For this to happen GHG emissions would need to be net zero by 2050 and, for that to happen, emissions need to be cut by 50% by 2030. Instead, rather than working towards this reduction pathway, the global economy emitted an additional 23 billion tons of CO_2 equivalent gases *above* the level needed to attain that net zero target (UNEP, 2022). The latest UNEP report on GHG reductions warns that even a 1.8-degree increase scenario "is currently not credible" (UNEP, 2022, p. XV). On top of this, recent studies of crucial geophysical systems, such as the Amazon rainforest and the arctic sea ice, indicate that previous research may have significantly underestimated the destabilizing impact of a 1.5-degree increase (Armstrong McKay et al., 2022; Wunderling, Donges, Kurths, & Winkelmann, 2021). The likelihood of cascading environmental consequences increases significantly with each incremental rise in global surface temperature. Despite these urgencies, achieving net zero emissions by 2050 is an immense task. The warnings of 30 years of reports from the IPCC have not impacted global emissions, and GHG emissions continue to rise every year. Even the brief hiatus afforded by the Covid-19 pandemic has now passed and emissions are now higher than ever (Ray, Singh, Singh, Acharya, & He, 2022).

What is rarely considered within these policy discussions is that reaching net zero emissions does not stop further damage to the atmosphere. The real task is to draw down the level of GHGs in the Earth's atmosphere to within a "safe operating space" (Rockström et al., 2009) that secures a stable and resilient climate. This will require a net *positive* drawdown of GHG. And it is not only with GHG emissions that we need to move beyond the ambition of 'net zero' targets. Earth Overshoot Day marks the date on which humanity's annual resource consumption exceeds Earth's capacity to regenerate those biological resources. In 2023 Earth Overshoot Day will fall on July 27. This means that, on an annual basis, humanity consumes twice as much as the planet can replace. For countries with highly industrialized economies their National Overshoot Day occurs significantly earlier in the year than those countries with lower levels of consumption. For much of the economically 'developed' world, Overshoot Day occurs in March or April. This means aiming for zero increase in carbon emissions or the consumption of natural resources will not restore the self-renewal capacities of Earth's biophysical systems. Achieving "Mission Zero" is like meeting the minimum repayments on a debt that is rapidly increasing. The same story can be told for biodiversity, ocean acidity, plastic pollution, and many other environmental problems. Merely aiming to stop more pollution, stop greater eutrophication of waterways, or conserve present levels of ecological resilience is not enough to return the Earth system to a stable state. We need to move beyond doing less harm or even no harm to the Earth's biophysical systems, but, rather positively, restore and regenerate the social-ecological systems that underpin all prosperity.

This is what regenerative sustainability aims for. It is not sufficient to set our sights on harm reduction or net zero to restoring the fundamental capacity of nature to regenerate itself and the human systems that depend on it. Regenerativity aims for the positive rejuvenation of nature and regenerative business aims to do this through the functioning of new forms of doing business. This is where a full and honest facing of the environmental facts opens us to the real possibility of doing things differently. To rejuvenate the ecological foundations of the planet, foundations that provide the necessary conditions for economic prosperity and human flourishing, it is imperative that a new melding of economic, social, and environmental values emerge in business. This book takes a deep dive into regenerative business and the actions and motivations of businesspeople who are voicing this new morality through striving to build regenerative organizations.

Regenerative sustainability

Regenerative sustainability is an ambitious form of sustainability that aims to go beyond "mission zero," or the goal of having a net neutral impact on the life-support capacities of natural systems. The intent is to positively contribute to a flourishing, abundant, and fertile biosphere with humanity as a constitutive aspect of nature rather than a controlling recipient of its "resources." This might appear to be a radical perspective, especially when considered in the context of conventional economic and business activities and goals. However, when seen with the context of the daunting facts of Earth system science, the notion of regenerativity becomes more understandable and normatively desirable.

Currently, although there is much discussion of sustainability and some important measures being taken by many at the firm level, globally the impact of economic growth policies continues to undermine the biophysical health of the planet. This gap between espoused goals and actual planetary impact has been called "the big disconnect" (Dyllick & Muff, 2016). The gap is broad and is still widening. In the meantime, the resilience of the planet's natural systems continues to be degraded to a point where many cannot recover without positive action. These failures demonstrate the necessity to rethink how business is done (Hahn & Tampe, 2021). The urgency and scale of societal transformation needed to ameliorate some of the worst impacts is increasing in both time and degree – meaning that there is increasingly less time to achieve ever greater levels of change. Hence, more ambitious forms of sustainability such as regenerativity are being discussed and acted on.

There is a significant and growing body of literature on the definition, theory, and practice of regenerative sustainability. We draw on this material to describe a few of these qualities. The intent here is to give a flavor of the regenerative perspective rather than an exhaustive account of its core aspects. There are several noteworthy features of a regenerative view of sustainability.

i)   *Sustainability-as-flourishing*: Regenerative businesses aim for flourishing forms of human community and natural life. Regenerativity goes beyond but includes the goals of minimizing harm, survival, preservation, or restoration to aim for a net positive impact on natural and social systems that results in "sustainability-as-flourishing" (Schaefer, Corner, & Kearins, 2015). This is an aspirational vision of planetary life where we see "radiant health, flourishing relationships, prospering enterprises, humming communities ... and a thriving natural environment" (Schaefer et al., 2015, p. 395). Regenerative sustainability starkly contrasts with the view of BAU activities augmented by incremental environmental and social business initiatives. While regenerativity involves an overall beneficial effect on social-ecological systems, there will inevitably be disruptive impacts at local or even regional levels that will need some form of redress. Regenerativity does not mean having no impact. Strategies to limit or balance negative impacts will be based on the specific needs of the socio-ecological systems in question.

ii) *Interdependency*: A regenerative understanding of sustainability sees people and nature as mutually co-creative and interdependent, with humanity being an integral aspect of an interconnected web of life. People impact on nature and are, in turn, shaped by those impacts. When people degrade Nature, we all suffer. When we respect Nature, and use its benefits wisely, we all flourish. Consequently, it matters as to the scope and scale of human environmental impacts on the biosphere in which it is embedded. Complexity/systems thinking capacities are intimately involved in both recognizing interdependency and responding appropriately.

iii) *Real Value*: Economic value is always more than monetary wealth. It is concerned with the well-being through the effective and efficient use of financial, social, cultural, ecological, and intellectual capital. The notion of "*real value*" (Sternad, Kennelly, & Bradley, 2016) includes economic, social, and environmental qualities but prioritizes social-ecological value over purely financial value. Regenerative sustainability sees the financial resources of an organization as a means for building up human and natural forms of capital rather than as its primary purpose.

iv) *Imagination*: Regenerativity values imagination and its application to real-world challenges. Creative imagination helps to build adaptive and transformative capabilities when the imperatives for change are urgent. Regenerativity is not a passive non-interference with nature but an adaptive and creative process of discovering ways to respect and learn from natural systems.

v) *Empowerment*: Regenerativity includes both social and environmental perspectives in sustainability transitions. A sustainable social-ecological system functions best when there is a prominent level of empowered participation of its members and groups. The capacity of members, stakeholders and rightholders to voice their interests and concerns contributes to the well-being of the whole. In unsustainable organizations, the rights of the few dominate over the well-being of the many, be they human or non-human forms of life. Sustainability transitions rely on collaborating for both social and environmental outcomes.

vi) *Technology and nature-based solutions*: Mainstream sustainability assumes technological solutions to be the main avenue for solving environmental crises. Regenerative sustainability flips this to emphasize nature-based solutions (NBS) with technology. NBS initiatives: i) focus on the protection, restoration, and/or regeneration of marine, terrestrial, and urban ecologies; ii) are inspired by nature to design solutions for grand challenges; iii) innovate to meet social needs while building up the resilience of ecological systems; iv) recognize the expertise of traditional and local communities and Indigenous peoples.

vii) *Intergenerational*: Temporal orientation is a definitive consideration for regenerative organizations. Whatever other elements are included, long-term and intergenerational timeframes are always an essential element in sustainability. As we will see in our cases, timeframes for regenerative projects are longer than conventional business initiatives.

These principles help to align the purpose and goals of regenerative organizations with the dynamics of a living planet. While all organizations will necessarily impact on natural systems and transform natural materials for its own use, these principles allow for ecosystems to retain their integrity, fundamental resilience, and capacity to regenerate what has been taken or disturbed for human purposes.

Business within planetary boundaries

One of the most powerful approaches to Earth system science is the Planetary Boundaries (PB) framework. The PB framework describes a set of nine biophysical global processes that enhance the conditions for life and enable atmospheric stability. The planetary processes include the climate system, oceans, the freshwater cycle, biodiversity, geo-biochemical flows (nutrient flows mostly from phosphorus and nitrogen), novel entities (such as plastics), land use, the ozone layer, and atmospheric aerosols. Empirical boundaries have been identified that demarcate the safe, increasing risk and high-risk zone and tipping point for most of these processes. Unfortunately, humanity, mostly through the impacts of global economic growth over the last 70 years, has pushed the Earth system into uncertain and high-risk zones for six of these nine areas. The planet is swiftly moving out of a "safe operating space for humanity" (Rockström et al., 2009). The framework is novel in that it empirically identifies the ecological and biophysical limits for a stable and resilient Earth system. Those empirical limits warn us of the risks involved in continuing with unsustainable economic activity. The PBs provide a scientific means for evaluating the impact of human activity on the health of ecological, atmospheric, oceanic, and terrestrial systems at the scale of the Earth system.

A simple metaphor follows that shows the usefulness of the PBs for thinking about global crises like climate change (see Figure 1.1). Let us take human body temperature as an example. Somewhere in the range 36°–37° Celsius is the standard body temperature for a person in good health. This temperature range demarcates the safe operating space for the vital process of maintaining human body temperature. Once the body temperature moves significantly beyond that range, problems emerge. Between 38° and 42° a person feels ill, and the body reacts by sweating, shivering, rapid breathing, changing heart rate, and circulation patterns. The person can take behavioral measures to reduce temperature by resting, taking medicine, using a damp cloth to cool the skin, adjusting the room temperature. Usually, a temperature of over 40° for an adult indicates a serious health emergency and medical professionals are called upon for assistance. Anything over 43° and death typically results. The increasing temperature points provide early warnings that a tipping point between life and death is approaching. At a certain empirically measurable point, the human system tips over from a state of life into fatal state of organ failure and system collapse. The same story holds for many other human systems. Changes in heart rates, blood pressures, levels of dehydration, blood sugar levels, and so on can all be measured and steps taken to address the warning signs.

This is analogous to the PB framework for measuring the health of the Earth system. For example, we know that for the case of climate change, anything over 350 parts per million (ppm) of CO_2 in the atmosphere will lead to a significant increase in the surface temperature of the planet and we enter the "increasing risk zone". Over 400 ppm (we are currently at 410 ppm) and we enter the high-risk zone. The high-risk zone is where

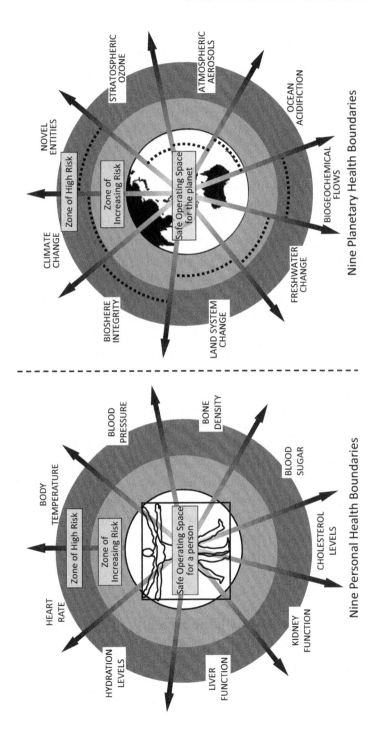

Figure 1.1 Personal and planetary health boundaries.

(Credit: Azote for Stockholm Resilience Centre, Stockholm University. Licenced under CC BYNC-ND 3.0 Based on Richardson et al. 2023, Steffen et al. 2015, and Rockström et al. 2009).

we begin triggering viral tipping points in many of the geophysical systems that enable planetary climactic stability. Human activity has resulted in the transgression of the increasing-risk boundaries for six of the nine PBs (Richardson et al., 2023). The Earth systems at increasing risk include biodiversity, climate, land system use, freshwater, biogeochemical flows (e.g., eutrophication of waterways due to excessive fertilizer use), and novel entities (e.g., plastics, toxic dumps). Net zero targets might have been appropriate thirty or forty years ago but not today. Aiming now for "net zero" harm to any of these fundamental planetary systems is not enough. When someone has a high temperature remedial action is needed. It is not enough to make sure they experience no additional harm. The Earth system is in need of immediate attention. We need a regenerative economy that restores the resilience and health to all of these planetary systems.

The nine PBs provide humanity with an early warning system for the health stability and fertility of the Earth system. The unhealthy relationship between economic activity and natural systems lies at the heart of all these worsening planetary problems. The author and entrepreneur Paul Hawken once said that "The first rule of sustainability is to align with natural forces, or at least not try to defy them". Based on Earth system science research programs such as the PB framework, we can say that the conventional approach to business is not only misaligned with natural forces but is also systematically degrading the life support networks that underpin the well-being of communities across the world. Social inequality often results from these misalignments. Subsistence and vulnerable communities who live close to the land are the first to feel the effects of unstable nature systems, be they extreme weather events, social conflicts, or reduced capacities for governance. Regenerative entrepreneurs are aware of these connections between nature and human communities and, consequently, they systematically include both environmental and social perspectives into the purposes, goals, and strategies of their business.

Doughnut Economics

Kate Raworth (2017) combined the PB framework with a set of social boundaries (derived from the Sustainable Development Goals – the SDGs) to create a framework called Doughnut Economics. This framework, shaped like a doughnut (see Figure 1.2), describes not only an environmentally

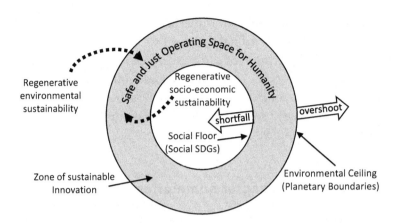

Figure 1.2 The Doughnut Economics model and regenerative sustainability.

safe operating space but also a socially just one. The outer boundary of the doughnut symbolizes the planetary boundaries or environmental ceiling, representing the limits to Earth's carrying capacity. As we have seen, operating within this boundary ensures a safe and environmentally sustainable future. The inner boundary symbolizes the social boundaries, or social floor/foundation, which represents the minimum social needs that prosperous human societies would provide to its citizens and communities (Raworth, 2017). Operating above the social floor and within the environmental ceiling creates a safe and just operating space, that is, a sustainable future for humanity. It is the task of businesses and organizations to ensure that their operations function within these needs and limits. These constraints support the creation of regenerative innovation. Regenerative innovation restores a safe and just operating space through creating goods and services that enable economies to re-enter this zone of social justice and environmental safety. Figure 1.2 shows the goal of regenerativity for both environmental and social sustainability. While all our cases aim for social and environmental regenerativity, some will take a special emphasis on one or other of these domains.

Nature is, of course, the most powerful force for environmental regeneration, but it needs time. The biosphere has recovered from several previous periods of severe degradation but did so only over immense time frames. Unfortunately, humanity does not have such a luxury (Vlasov, 2021). We need to learn from nature to facilitate the process of regeneration. Life on Earth has been an ongoing process of natural "research and development," as the biomimicry entrepreneur Janine Benyus (1997) puts it, and we would be wise to draw on natural designs if we are to develop truly regenerative economies. Enterprises of all kinds are needed to contribute to these transformational transitions. The coming decades offer the greatest opportunity for business to collaborate with the public section, Non-Government Organizations (NGOs), social enterprises, and international bodies to actively repair, and restore, the biosphere.

Chapter summaries

In this book we take four stories of organizations, and their founding and guiding entrepreneurs, as illustrative case studies for understanding the role of values in regenerative sustainability. We selected our cases using criteria based on the definitive qualities of regenerative businesses discussed above and on other considerations such as variety in organizational form, for example, for-profit and community-based, and what those organizations produced, for example, commercial products and educational services. The cases all share the core purpose of contributing to regenerative forms of sustainability, but they do so through a diverse range of organizational forms and activities which offer many rich perspectives for exploring the expression of values in quite different contexts. Table 1.1 presents the case organizations and their characteristics, including year of foundation, the number of members or employees, their regenerative purpose, the form of the organization and its products/services.

Using the seven GVV pillars as our navigating compass, we explore how an action-based understanding of ethics sheds light on how the founders and business leaders of these four organizations express their core values to effect real change. These are positive stories of how opportunities for addressing major business challenges were recognized and taken up to add regenerative value to human communities and the ecological systems on which they depend. In the past, GVV has most commonly been applied to the resolution of ethical challenges and values conflicts in the workplace. In the following chapters we look more into the opportunities that arise when voicing values leads to new visions, solutions, technologies, and social innovations. This application of GVV to regenerative sustainability is not only relevant to the firm-level entrepreneur and the adding of sustainable value to local communities, but also has implications for how

Table 1.1 Characteristics of the case organizations

Case organization	Year Founded	No. of members/employees	Regenerative purpose	Organizational form	Products/Services
Earth Regenerators (Chapter 3)	2020	105 employees 4,000 members	"A study and activism group for restoring planetary health and avoiding human extinction"	Not-for-Profit international community network	Educational services, networking opportunities knowledge sharing
Commonland (Chapter 4)	2013	19 employees	"Building a balance between ecology, economics and hope" the returns (natural returns) social returns, financial returns, and inspirational returns.	Not-for-profit international enterprise	Regenerated natural landscapes, human communities, and economic opportunities.
Individuell Människohjälp & Humanium Metal (Chapter 5)	2016	IM - c. 6,000 (members) HM – 10 (employees)	"upcycling a commodity for killing into a commodity for peace" "creating a platform for a global peace and security."	Not-for-Profit international development organization	High quality consumer products, community development, opportunities for youth.
The Seaweed Company (Chapter 6)	2018	30 employees	"To safeguard a liveable future for ourselves and our children for generations to come."	For-Profit company	Regenerative seaweed products for global applications

economies and societies tackle the global social-ecological challenges that we currently face.

Throughout the book we have adopted an appreciative stance towards our cases and entrepreneurs. Appreciative in the sense of aiming to understand and respect the perspectives presented, the values expressed, and the forms of expression. Each organization described in the following pages is offering a considered response to the growing impacts of global environmental crises on both human and non-human communities. In legal structure, the organizations examined include a for-profit business, a social enterprise consisting of a foundation and development company, a membership-based international aid organization, and a volunteer-based community organization. These organizations represent a wide range of values, ideas, and perspectives, but they all publicly identify as having a regenerative purpose. We do not critically assess the validity of these viewpoints but describe the visions and values held by regenerative organizations and entrepreneurs and appreciatively explore how and why they are expressed. The aim is to communicate insights into how sustainability leaders develop and express their values through regenerative business ventures, and we use the GVV perspective to uncover these insights.

The course of the book runs as follows. In this current chapter we describe the rationale for the book and provide an overview of regenerative sustainability and why it is needed. In Chapter 2 we introduce our approach by presenting the basic elements of GVV and its innovative orientation towards business ethics. We will also present here some distinctive features of GVV that we emphasize in studying our four cases. Chapter 3 presents the case of Earth Regenerators and the social entrepreneurs Joe Brewer and J.P. Parker. Earth Regenerators is a global community-based organization that works on the radical edge of deep sustainability transitions. We use the GVV pillars of *Values* and *Choice* to explore examining the approach that Earth Regenerators takes towards radical transformation. In Chapter 4, the social business Commonland is described, and we apply the pillar of *Normalizing* to delve into how this visionary business and its founder, Willem, and its director of innovation, Simon, are working to make the Commonland approach more accepted across the land management and land care sectors. These entrepreneurs and their colleagues are shifting the way stakeholders view the relationship between business, society, and nature and

how that vision inspires new economic opportunities. The Swedish coop-
erative development organization Individuell Människohjälp (IM), and its
offshoot social enterprise Humanium Metal, are the subjects of Chapter 5.
This case focuses on the social dimension of regenerativity and, because
the personal drivers of professional purpose and a sense of responsibility are so evident in this case, we use the pillars of *Self-story* and *Purpose*.
Our entrepreneurs, Simon and Jacqueline, were both involved in the initial
piloting of Humanium Metal and are currently its core business managers.
The for-profit business, The Seaweed Company, is the case up for analysis in
Chapter 6. The Seaweed Company is a private company that is competing on
open international markets and so encounters all the powerful reasons for
adopting conventional business strategies. How it manages to thrive, provide regenerative solutions, and overcome inhibiting arguments that often
silence sustainability values is the focal theme of this chapter. The *Voice* and
Rationalizations pillars were explicitly chosen to explore the approaches of the
company's founder and "SeaEO" (Joost) and its Commerce Lead (Wouter).
Chapter 7 sets out our insights and key findings and draws together the key
themes of the book to see how ethics and values contribute to regenerative
entrepreneuring and sustainability transitioning.

How to use this book

Regenerative Business Voices has been written with a broad range of readers in
mind. Those who are interested in regenerative sustainability, new kinds
of organizational purpose, or leading-edge forms of entrepreneurship will
find much to explore. While business ethics is a key focus, it should not be
assumed that only students or business leaders interested in ethics will find
this book useful. The approach taken to ethics here is that moral capacities
are fundamental to all aspects of doing business. Sustainability is no longer
an optional or peripheral dimension of doing business; rather, it defines
the very essence of what good business and business leadership is all about.
Whether you are a student or in a leadership role, an innovator, work in
communications and community relations, finances, sales or recruitment
and staff development you will find aspects of these cases that speak to
you. We intend this exploration of regenerativity and business ethics to
be an inspiring, empowering, and useful guide for business practitioners,

the general audience and anyone interested in innovative approaches to sustainability.

Each of the case chapters follows a similar structure. They begin with a case description and a brief biographical outline of the two entrepreneurs that played a pivotal role in establishing and running the organization. Next, we provide a description and appreciative analysis of the entrepreneurs' actions in such areas as stakeholder engagements, the application of corporate values, strategic decision-making, vision building and communication. We perform this analysis using the GVV pillars that we find to be most applicable to the relevant business case (see further details in the chapter summaries above). Following the analysis, we describe important insights and implications gained through the GVV analysis of the cases. We hope these insights give some direction for debating and discussing the cases, their implications for regenerative sustainability, and the general process of transitioning towards sustainability futures. Finally, each chapter ends with several learning exercises and case questions that can be adapted to different educational settings. A detailed description of the exercises is provided to support their use in the classroom. We hope these additional materials help teachers and facilitators explore the applied usefulness of the topics raised in the chapter. In summary, each of the case chapters follows this structure: i) case description and entrepreneur biographies, ii) GVV analysis, iii) insights and implications, and iv) learning exercises and case questions.

Apart from the inherently interesting nature of these stories, the book can create learning opportunities for various audiences. The cases provide rich material for debate and discussion and the exercises at the end of each case chapter can be used to explore many ethics and sustainability topics in greater depth. These exercises are suitable for a wide range of classroom settings and can be adapted to undergraduate, postgraduate, and executive education settings for both classroom and online learning. We have intended that the chapters also deal with sustainability skills across a diverse range of competencies, including areas such as ethics, interpersonal relations, strategy, complexity and systems thinking, and anticipatory competencies. Business students and educators need resources for analyzing and practicing the competencies involved in emerging forms of organizational sustainability and the chapters that follow contain many examples for discussion and practice in this important field.

Notes

1 Functional biodiversity refers to the behavioral "work" that species do in maintaining ecosystems and in the ecosystems services they provide to humanity, for example, pollination, medicines, food sources, etc. Functional biodiversity has been greatly reduced because of the massive reduction in animal populations in recent years.
2 Genetic biodiversity refers to the variety of the genetic wealth of diverse species. This is typically thought of as the numbers of extinct, endangered and threatened species.

References

Almond, R. E. A., Grooten, M., Juffe Bignoli, D., & Petersen, T. (Eds.). (2022). *Living Planet Report 2022: Building a Nature Positive Society*. Gland, Switzerland: WWF (Worldwide Fund for Nature).

Armstrong McKay, D. I., Staal, A., Abrams, J. F., Winkelmann, R., Sakschewski, B., Loriani, S., ... Lenton, T. M. (2022). Exceeding 1.5°C global warming could trigger multiple climate tipping points. *Science*, 377(6611), 7950. doi:10.1126/science.abn7950

Austin, J. L. (1975). *How to Do Things with Words*. Oxford: Oxford University Press.

Barnosky, A. D., Matzke, N., Tomiya, S. U. G. O., Wogan, B., Swartz, T. B., ... Maguire, K. C. (2011). Has the Earth's sixth mass extinction already arrived? *Nature, 471*, 51–57.

Benyus, J. M. (1997). *Biomimicry: Innovation Inspired by Nature*. New York: Morrow.

Butler, J. (1997). *Excitable Speech: A Politics of the Performative*. London: Routledge.

Cowie, R. H., Bouchet, P., & Fontaine, B. (2022). The sixth mass extinction: Fact, fiction or speculation? *Biological Reviews*, 97(2), 640–663. doi:10.1111/brv.12816

Dyllick, T., & Muff, K. (2016). Clarifying the meaning of sustainable business: Introducing a typology from business-as-usual to true business sustainability. *Organization & Environment*, 29(2), 156–174. doi:10.1177/1086026615575176

Elhacham, E., Ben-Uri, L., Grozovski, J., Bar-On, Y. M., & Milo, R. (2020). Global human-made mass exceeds all living biomass. *Nature, 588*(7838), 442–444.

Gaffney, O., & Steffen, W. (2017). The Anthropocene equation. *The Anthropocene Review, 4*(1), 53–61.

Garry, R. F. (2022). The evidence remains clear: SARS-CoV-2 emerged via the wildlife trade. *Proceedings of the National Academy of Sciences, 119*(47), e2214427119. doi:10.1073/pnas.2214427119

Gibb, R., Redding, D. W., Chin, K. Q., Donnelly, C. A., Blackburn, T. M., Newbold, T., & Jones, K. E. (2020). Zoonotic host diversity increases in human-dominated ecosystems. *Nature.* doi:10.1038/s41586-020-2562-8

Hahn, T., & Tampe, M. (2021). Strategies for regenerative business. *Strategic Organization, 19*(3), 456–477.

IPCC, Shukla, P. R., Skea, J., Slade, R., Khourdajie, A. A., Diemen, R. V., ... Malley, J. (Eds.). (2022). *Climate Change 2022: Mitigation of Climate Change. Contribution of Working Group III to the Sixth Assessment Report of the Intergovernmental Panel on Climate Change: Summary for Policymakers.* Cambridge, UK: Cambridge University Press.

Keesing, F., & Ostfeld, R. S. (2021). Impacts of biodiversity and biodiversity loss on zoonotic diseases. *Proceedings of the National Academy of Sciences, 118*(17), e2023540118. doi:10.1073/pnas.2023540118

Li, Q., England, M. H., Hogg, A. M., Rintoul, S. R., & Morrison, A. K. (2023). Abyssal ocean overturning slowdown and warming driven by Antarctic meltwater. *Nature, 615*(7954), 841–847. doi:10.1038/s41586-023-05762-w

Pekar, J. E., Magee, A., Parker, E., Moshiri, N., Izhikevich, K., Havens, J. L., ... Wertheim, J. O. (2022). The molecular epidemiology of multiple zoonotic origins of SARS-CoV-2. *Science, 377*(6609), 960–966. doi:10.1126/science.abp8337

Plotnikof, M., & Mumby, D. K. (2023). Temporal multimodality and performativity: Exploring politics of time in the discursive, communicative constitution of organization. *Organization.* https://journals.sagepub.com/doi/abs/10.1177/13505084221145649

Plowright, R. K., Reaser, J. K., Locke, H., Woodley, S. J., Patz, J. A., Becker, D. J., ... Tabor, G. M. (2021). Land use-induced spillover: A call to action to safeguard environmental, animal, and human health. *The Lancet Planetary Health, 5*(4), e237–e245. doi:10.1016/S2542-5196(21)00031-0

Raworth, K. (2017). *Doughnut Economics: Seven Ways to Think Like a 21st-Century Economist.* London: Chelsea Green Publishing.

Ray, R. L., Singh, V. P., Singh, S. K., Acharya, B. S., & He, Y. (2022). What is the impact of COVID-19 pandemic on global carbon emissions? *Science of The Total Environment, 816,* 151503. doi:10.1016/j.scitotenv.2021.151503

Richardson, K., Steffen, W., Lucht, W., Bendtsen, J., Cornell, S. E., Donges, J. F., ... Rockström, J. (2023). Earth beyond six of nine planetary boundaries. *Science Advances, 9*(37), eadh2458. doi:10.1126/sciadv.adh2458

Rockström, J., Steffen, W., Noone, K., Persson, Å.F., Stuart Chapin, I., Lambin, E. F., ... Foley, J. A. (2009). A safe operating space for humanity. *Nature, 461*(7263), 472–475.

Schaefer, K., Corner, P., & Kearins, K. (2015). Social, environmental and sustainable entrepreneurship research: What is needed for sustainability-as-flourishing? *Organization & Environment, 28.* doi:10.1177/1086026615621111

Spalding, C., & Hull, P. M. (2021). Towards quantifying the mass extinction debt of the Anthropocene. *Proceedings of the Royal Society B: Biological Sciences, 288*(1949), 20202332. doi:10.1098/rspb.2020.2332

Steffen, W., Broadgate, W., Deutsch, L., Gaffney, O., & Ludwig, C. (2015). The trajectory of the Anthropocene: The great acceleration. *The Anthropocene Review, 2*(1), 81–98.

Sternad, D., Kennelly, J. J., & Bradley, F. (2016). *Digging Deeper: How Purpose-Driven Enterprises Create Real Value.* Austin, TX: Greenleaf.

UNEP. (2022). *Emissions Gap Report 2022: The Closing Window – Climate Crisis Calls for Rapid Transformation of Societies.* Retrieved from Nairobi: https://www.unep.org/emissions-gap-report-2022

United Nations. (2022). *Secretary-General Warns of Climate Emergency.* Retrieved from https://press.un.org/en/2022/sgsm21228.doc.htm

Vlasov, M. (2021). In transition toward the ecocentric entrepreneurship nexus: How nature helps entrepreneurs make ventures more regenerative over time. *Organization & Environment, 34*(4), 559–580.

Worley, C. G., & Jules, C. (2020). COVID-19's uncomfortable revelations about agile and sustainable organizations in a VUCA world. *The Journal of Applied Behavioral Science, 56*(3), 279–283. doi:10.1177/0021886320936263

Worobey, M., Levy, J. I., Serrano, L. M., Crits-Christoph, A., Pekar, J. E., Goldstein, S. A., ... Andersen, K. G. (2022a). The Huanan Seafood Wholesale Market in Wuhan was the early epicenter of the COVID-19 pandemic. *Science.* doi:10.1126/science.abp8715

Worobey, M., Levy, J. I., Serrano, L. M. M., Crits-Christoph, A., Pekar, J. E., Goldstein, S. A., ... Andersen, K. G. (2022b). The Huanan market was the epicenter of SARS-CoV-2. doi:10.5281/zenodo.6299600

Wunderling, N., Donges, J. F., Kurths, J., & Winkelmann, R. (2021). Interacting tipping elements increase risk of climate domino effects under global warming. *Earth System Dynamics*, *12*(2), 601–619. doi:10.5194/esd-12-601-2021

2

GIVING VOICE TO
REGENERATIVE VALUES

In this chapter we describe Mary Gentile's business ethics approach, called "Giving Voice to Values" (GVV), and discuss its relevance for investigating regenerative business sustainability and entrepreneurship. Much has been written about GVV and, while a comprehensive description of the approach will not be presented here, we will outline its core features and highlight those most relevant to our topic of regenerative sustainability. The 7 pillars and 12 assumptions that define GVV provide a powerful skill-based framework for analysing the micro-foundational processes that underpin an organization's ethical culture. As such, it is eminently suited to the topic of sustainability transitions. Organizational sustainability is concerned with change, and the purpose and direction of transitioning to more sustaining and sustainable states of organizing. Among other shared domains of interest, it is these normative topics of directionality and purpose that connect the topics of sustainability and ethics at their core.

DOI: 10.4324/9781003330660-2

"What if we were to act on our values"

It is no exaggeration to say that "Giving Voice to Values" (GVV) has reshaped the way ethics is taught and communicated in business and management schools, corporations, and community settings across the world. GVV is both a theory and a pedagogy initially developed by Mary Gentile (2010a, 2010b, 2017) and developed through subsequent research and teaching (Arce & Gentile, 2014; Edwards & Kirkham, 2014; Miller & Shawver, 2021; Shawver & Miller, 2021). GVV emphasizes the power of moral imagination and the active expression of core values in developing ethical organizational cultures. In contrast to many other business ethics approaches, GVV engages with the need for ethical organizations, not by thinking about rules, not by equivocating over whether to do something or not, not by calculating the costs, but by doing, by initiating action. All these other aspects of awareness, judgement, decision-making and motivation can follow, but GVV respects the initial movement of taking action, voicing concerns, and enacting possibilities. GVV asks the question: "What if we were going to act on our values—what would we say and do?" (Gentile, 2010a, p. 28). The GVV pedagogy provides sophisticated guidelines for responding to this values-based inquiry, for example, in finding supports for acting on values and methods for improving levels of skill, self-efficacy, and determination.

GVV moves well beyond conversations about what is right or wrong by exercising capacities for actionable dialogue. The purpose is to enhance individuals' ability to enact their values, express their opinions, and develop action plans to deal with ethical challenges. The metaphor of 'giving voice' includes multiple forms of expressions, such as asking well-framed and well-timed questions, gathering and sharing data, building coalitions, finding allies, identifying stakeholders, clarifying purpose, crafting responses, speaking quietly behind the scenes with relevant people, and listening to the concerns of stakeholders. GVV promotes proactivity and innovation rather than reactivity and regulation and allows individuals to experiment with ways of giving voice to values more effectively. It can be distinguished from other action-based approaches as it takes into consideration the personal stories and preferences of ethical actors. As we will see in the following cases, you do not have to be a hero, extrovert, or oratory genius to discover your own voice and be skilful in how you apply it to creatively resolve ethical problems or opportunities.

While GVV is primarily directed to the personal position of "what will I say and do" it is inherently intersubjective and social in that giving voice assumes the social context of conversation, dialogue, persuasion, and the articulation of shared values that constitute an organization's ethical climate. Multicultural research has found that most people share some core values, such as honesty, respect, responsibility, fairness, and compassion (Donaldson & Dunfee, 1994; Sagiv, Roccas, Cieciuch, & Schwartz, 2017; Schwartz & Bardi, 2001). While these core values might be relatively few in number, they can be manifested in an infinite variety of ways. They can be prioritized differently, result in different preferences, and be expressed through a multitude of cultural meanings and symbols. For all their variety of expression, however, if the goodwill is there, core values can provide an orienting moral compass that guides conversations and communications across any difference. Skill and ethical competency in expressing and engaging in values-based conversations is the key factor here. Hence, recognizing the shared nature of core values supports conversations to decide moral choices and take hold of ethical opportunities (Gentile, 2010a). GVV comes within an important but pedagogically underutilized lineage of ethics approaches that highlight the power of communicative practices.[1] Communication is seen as the primary means for creating organizational climate and culture and facilitating ethical behavior. This is especially so for supporting transformative change such as sustainability transitions.

Sustainability competencies and regenerative values

Sustainability is about normative change; it involves reflection on where we have been and where we are headed and changing course as needed. Sustainability transitions are system changes that organizations and economies plan for and implement. Transitions can be deep and involve transformative, qualitative shifts in the entire system or shallow and aim for incremental, quantitative changes in defined parts of a system. The normative nature of sustainability means that it requires a defined purpose, a goal that describes something better than the status quo. Consequently, it necessarily involves the development and setting of a vision, communicating that vision, building collaborations, developing technical capacities, and highlighting the role of guiding values and social practices. Regenerative sustainability recognizes the need for reconnecting what has been previously set apart – reconnecting businesses with nature and the biosphere, reconnecting people by appreciating their diverse backgrounds, perspectives, and competencies, reconnecting technologies with the human benefits they are meant to support. Doing any of this involves ethical considerations. Undertaking regenerative sustainability transitions means reflecting on the role of values, thinking about how a business' purpose is aligned with its actual impact on stakeholders and the extended stakeholder circle of suppliers, customers, host communities, and the natural systems that support them.

The personal and organizational capacities needed for successfully navigating sustainability transitions can be broadly categorized into four skill sets (see Figure 2.1). One set is technical skills, the 'hard' skills involving disciplines such as engineering, technology development, digitalization, metrics, and measurement. Another set is social skills, the various 'soft' skills including anticipatory, normative, interpersonal, strategy, complexity/systems thinking, and change management competencies. Social competencies in sustainability management refer to the coordination of necessary but often invisible or intangible dimensions of organizing and managing change. These skills are better thought of as the social and interpersonal infrastructure that scaffolds and enables any material or technological infrastructure, production process, or product. Intra-personal skills might also be included here in that self-knowledge and self-awareness are

Figure 2.1 Skill sets for managing sustainability transitions.

important qualities for navigating any change process. A third set is financial skills of budgetary control, financial reporting, and investment which often interface between the technical and the social. And finally, there is the set of co-ordinating skills group needed for the integration of each of these – the technical, the economic and the social/interpersonal.

Unfortunately, these skill sets are often haphazardly combined and applied without any thought about how they interact to create the right conditions for sustainability transitions. This is particularly true for socio-cultural skills, which are frequently neglected in favor of a technical focus on target goals. In other words, the social infrastructure of mindsets, strategies, cultural preparedness, interpersonal and ethical competencies, all those social skills that scaffold change, are often neglected or, at least, undervalued. Instead, the economic and technical dimensions take the center stage and are resourced and budgeted for. The reduction of sustainability to technical metrics is one of the reasons there has been so little movement in the deep transitioning of the global economy. We have known for many years that addressing climate change for example, requires massive systems-level transformation and yet no net global reduction in atmospheric CO_2, nor any improvement in the collapse of biodiversity, has yet been observed. One of the reasons for this "big disconnect" (Dyllick & Muff, 2016) is the reliance on technical metrics and the neglect of ethical commitments to transformative goals. Values play an essential role in coordinating complex skills and for explaining the lack of coordinated action when they are neglected as in the indecisiveness over climate change action. In the following chapters we focus on this ethics and values side of the change equation. We explore the 'soft' social competencies of regenerative sustainability transitions through the lens of ethical commitments and guiding values.

Special attention will be paid to the *coordinating skills* that integrate the social with other dimensions of sustainability. This coordinating competency can be illustrated by the following. It has been noted that hi-tech, manufacturing, and building companies concentrate on environmental sustainability because they have the disciplinary expertise to focus on technical and engineering skills in achieving their sustainability goals (Labuschagne, Brent, & van Erck, 2005; Mies & Gold, 2021). Environmental sustainability is frequently reduced to metrics about energy and materials use, hence engineering skills are taken to be most relevant. In contrast, service industries often focus on the social sustainability dimensions of cultural and gender diversity, empowered workplace environments, and flexible working conditions but are often weak on the environmental sustainability side. These are systematic biases in how companies perceive and address sustainability depending on their industrial culture. Integrative competencies are important to address these kinds of weaknesses and integrative approaches to combing social and environmental sustainability goals can be beneficial for both. For example, developing both technical and social infrastructures can determine the success or failure of implementing circular economy strategies. Circular business innovations need various kinds of supporting infrastructures to work well. One of the following cases, Humanium Metal, provides a powerful illustration of how "regenerative recycling" (Poponi, Colantoni, Cividino, & Mosconi, 2019) requires intense coordination of individual and group aptitudes and skills, financial resources, technological infrastructures, planning capacities, and so on. To do this well people need to be heard. Stakeholders need to trust that both their concerns and their innovative inspirations will be acted on if they are voiced. This notion of *voice* is the capacity for individual and collective stakeholders to express (and hear) values and it is one of the definitive features, or pillars, of GVV. The following section provides an overview of the 12 assumptions and 7 GVV pillars.

The 12 assumptions

GVV builds on some underlying assumptions about the purpose, process, and implications of expressing core values. The assumptions include common and well-established ideas that, for example (the following is a selection of the 12 assumptions, for a full description see Gentile, 2010a): i) people want to express their core values and have experience of doing so, ii) expressing values is a skill that can be learned and improved, iii) situational factors deeply affect the expression of core values, iv) practice increases self-confidence, engages moral imagination, and supports the sense of responsibility, v) engaging in values-based conversations is crucial for overcoming moral silence, and vi) finding allies can help people express their values.

All the 12 assumptions relate to taking action, that is, to saying or doing something regarding an ethical challenge or opportunity. The GVV assumptions can be seen as performative principles because action creates the social conditions that support the emergence of ethical awareness, moral judgements, and decision-making. The concept of performativity is the idea that activity mediates changes in thinking, feeling, and identity. What we do and say is constitutive of our ethical and moral identities. The GVV assumptions are infused with the idea that language and conversation are not just means for conveying information but also ways of building moral identity. Practices play a significant role in performative ethics because they are behaviors that have become routinized and, hence, the means for building an organization's ethical culture. It is through embedded practices that individuals and groups express and reinforce their core values and ethical commitments.

As used here, performative action is not to be equated with a perfunctory or superficial performance. This pejorative use of the term *performative* refers to the managerial world of control, performance management, and worker productivity (see, for example, Jones et al., 2020). We use the term in its original sense of the practice of shaping personal and social realities through the action of speech (see, for example, Austin, 1975; Blok, 2013). Performative in this sense means to bring a possibility into existence. The performative nature of language not only describes something but *does* something. The 12 assumptions of GVV are not just descriptive, they are performative in that they assume the act of "voicing" changes things. We will describe some of these assumptions and then give some practical examples to describe this performative aspect of GVV.

It is assumed in GVV that people have a small number of shared values, basic principles that guide them toward achieving their dreams and ultimate purposes. Each person inherently wants to "voice", express, and act on these core values. But it is harder to do this in some situations than in others, especially if we do not practice the skill of voicing our values. The better we know ourselves and the more we try to be who we are at our best, the more we will act on and express our values in pragmatic and skilful ways. For example, a key assumption is that all this results in the possibility of better decision-making for a community. Furthermore, the more those positive outcomes are recognized, the more likely it is that we subsequently enact our values and voice our concerns and commitments. Silence and inaction, in contrast, fertilize the conditions for unethical behavior, toxic leadership, or unsustainable business practices. When the values of the many are muted or go unarticulated, the values of the status quo or few get to decide how the future unfolds. When the everyday function of social systems, organizations, and businesses require that people be silent, that is when the unethical, the autocratic, or the merely mundane flourish.

There are powerful performative connections between the personal availability to speak freely and collective freedoms. The adage that evil flourishes when good people are silent captures well this aspect of GVV. These assumptions promote a perspective that diverse opinions need to be heard, even when they might cause discomfort. At the same time, however, GVV aims to help folks find ways to express these views in ways that make it easier for others to truly hear them. Healthy forms of consultative democracy emerge from these micro-foundations of respecting diverse voices whether we agree with them or not. This does not mean condoning speech that incites or threatens violence or material harm, but it does mean creating social environments that welcome contrarian views. Together, these assumptions form a set of tenets that support an action-based method for organizational capacity building called in GVV the "7 pillars". In the following case chapters, we use these pillars as analytical lenses for exploring how entrepreneurs voice their values to create regenerative organizations.

The 7 pillars

The 7 pillars or foundational concepts that ground the GVV pedagogy describe not only a conceptual framework for supporting a skills-based understanding of business ethics, but also a method for acting, for putting values into practice.

Values (knowing yourself and your values)

The first of the 7 GVV pillars is *Values*. Values are the broad principles that guide us toward our purpose. They "serve as guiding principles in people's lives" (Sagiv et al., 2017, p. 630) and are broad in that they cut across situational and social boundaries. Values are personal commitments that we hold internally rather than being rules that are imposed on us from the outside. Our values are part of us, they are not codes that we follow but aspirations that we choose to enact. Where our values are the main means by which we assess worth or quality, the value of something is the explicit importance of that thing, process, or event when it is socially exchanged. When we give expression to our values, we make the implicit explicit and engage with the social world of valuation. Hence, GVV is not just a private exercise. Giving voice to our concerns and dreams contributes our own attitudes and intentions into the social task of assessing what is valuable and worthwhile in life. The motivational impulse here is to close the gap between who we are now and who we want to become. Core values help us follow a pathway for *doing* that.

In contrast to common understandings of ethics, values are commitments that we have internalized and made personal. Rather than the unfortunate, but often held, view of ethics as an externally imposed code of regulations enforced by authoritarian sanctions, GVV frames ethics as the process of discovering "our deepest sense of who we wish to be" (Gentile, 2010a) and business ethics as the collective dimension of that journey undertaken in organizational life. Business ethics from this perspective is about the search for excellence, for maximizing purpose, and for practicing values that help us flourish together through our work. The definitive qualities of regenerative sustainability, as outlined in Chapter 1, align well with this GVV understanding of ethics and values. The notions of positive regeneration, interdependency, and participatory empowerment exemplify the GVV orientation of values as both personal and interpersonal guides for action. Regenerative values clearly resonate with the core values of respect, compassion, and responsibility. What regenerative values add is, first, that they prioritize social-ecological systems in the exercising of care and the estimation of value, and second, that these commitments are operative over intergenerational timeframes. Regenerativity involves commitments not just for the short term of annual quarters or even midterm 2–5-year planning periods. Regenerative values have inherent integrity in that they guide commitments irrespective of intermittent fluctuations in markets, investment bubbles, or consumer fads.

In speaking of values, distinctions can be made between core values, situational or utilitarian values, and preferences. Core values are our deepest ethical commitments to qualities such as honesty, respect, compassion, justice, loyalty, and responsibility. Core values might be regarded as hypernorms (Donaldson & Dunfee, 1994) which help to coordinate more localized, situational values. Situational values appear in various local contexts, such as home, work, social leisure, and institutional settings. In such settings, qualities such as punctuality, hospitality, reliability, generosity, and resourcefulness are often regarded as useful and desirable. You can see that situational values quickly multiply from the small set of core values as different settings are adapted to. Similarly, personal preferences can be regarded as the multiplicity of characteristics that guide our preferential choices. While the array of situational values and preferences are unique to each individual and may or may not be commonly held by others, core values are shared across many cultures, contexts, and contingencies. From the GVV perspective, voicing *values* means expressing these shared core values in some way. Expressing a value can be done variously through conversation, social media, text, or artistic activity but it will always refer to a core ethical commitment. Voicing values is the interpersonal or public sharing of those ideas that guide us toward the central goals we have in life.

Choice (believing you have a choice to voice your values)

Feeling that you have the personal power to choose between alternative responses to an ethical challenge constitutes the pillar of Choice in the GVV approach. Where values guide and steer us toward our main purpose, the pillar of choice is the power source, the engine that drives a sense of self-efficacy to move along that journey. Choice is exercised the more we believe that we have a choice. In this sense GVV is a performative approach to ethics (Edwards & Kirkham, 2014) in that it is through (per-) the action (-form) that ethical value is realized. Stepping into possibility by acting and expressing our interests and then reflecting on how well we did or how we might have done it otherwise, is the basis for acquiring ethical skills and moral strength. We have all expressed our values under both favorable and difficult circumstances at some point and reflecting on the factors that helped or hindered us can be a powerful source of ethical learning. Gentile points out that identifying these enabling and inhibiting factors can be the most powerful means for pragmatically addressing ethics issues in the workplace.

> Why do we choose to voice and act on our values when we do? And how can we build the confidence and skills and determination to do so more often? Recognizing the fact that we are all capable of speaking and acting on our values, as well as the fact that we have not always done so, is both empowering and enlightening. It is perhaps the most important of the ways of thinking about values in the workplace.
>
> (Gentile, 2010a)

A sense of choice is a key quality in working toward sustainable economic and business futures. As mentioned previously, sustainability is a normative endeavor, meaning that it aims to move toward a better future, a normative vision where we pass over to the next generation a world that is in better economic, social, and ecological condition than that which we inherited. Although the picture is complex, this is not what is happening currently. It is true that in recent decades great economic wealth has been created and many millions of people across the world have lifted themselves out of economic poverty, but this has come at immense social and environmental cost. The current system for creating wealth has undermined the environmental basis for its continuation. Environmental and Earth system science tells us that current economic practices are unsustainable. The reasonable and prudent response here is to transform our approach to economic production and consumption. We must change our global and national economic systems to ones based on the sustainable practices of a regenerative economy rather than the unsustainable practices of an extractive economy. Choice and the capacity for imagination that generates choice, lie at the heart of any move toward sustainable alternatives. We need to choose economic pathways to sustainable futures that: i) recognize the urgency for transformation, ii) can imagine doing things differently, iii) look to regenerative businesses that are successfully operating now, iv) experiment with market-based mechanisms for regenerative transformation. The notion of choice is tightly linked to each of these steps. There is no need for choice in a perfectly functioning system. But when things go awry, imagination and choice become critical for changing course toward something better.

Normalization (seeing ethical challenges as normal aspects of doing business)

An important observation in GVV is that ethical challenges are everyday aspects of organizational life. Ethical choices occur regularly because there are always opportunities for improving the business cultures in which we work. Interpersonal conflicts, opportunities for expressing one's values, creating possibilities for innovation, these are all part of the daily drama of workplaces, whether online or in person. Conventional business ethics often represent ethical challenges and dilemmas as rare and unexpected events. This view is not only inaccurate, but it also hinders proactive approaches to ethical capacity building. The enactment of moral commitments and values-based judgements is an ongoing aspect of life in general, and work in particular. Making a profit is a moral goal. Introducing a sustainability strategy is a values-based decision. Because ethics is inherent to organizing for such goals and making such judgements, businesses and leaders need to be aware of their values and deliberative in implementing them. A business that is not ethically deliberative and responds unconsciously and reactively to ethical problems is itself a fundamental ethical problem.

Organizational leaders who assume ethical situations are rare or random events typically create organizational climates that have weaknesses in other domains. First, cultures of discrimination, harassment, and even abuse flourish whenever the voices of stakeholders are not heard or acted on. Normalizing moral choices as daily occurrences means that a resilient culture of candor and awareness can flourish rather than one of denial and silence. Second, innovation culture suffers. The same forces that resist the free expression of values also inhibit the expression of new ideas. For example, a sense of psychological safety is needed to build an innovation culture that allows for failure in the quest for developing new services or for improving the quality of old ones. Third, the view that moral challenges are rare creates the impression that things are fine just the way they are. A culture of avoidance does not look for, or see, the signs of impending change. Normalizing the ethical dimension of any decision creates the preparatory conditions for adaptation and transformation. Fourth, assuming the assemblage of standard procedures and practices as the norm and ethical issues as rare means that leaders and managers are not prepared for them when they do happen. Staff can be "at a loss" in such instances. Not knowing what to do, they just try to get everything back to "normal". In the context of sustainability, all this adds up to the defence of the 'status quo' and the denial of the need for transformative change. Rather than an anticipatory culture of foresight, forms of reactive leadership that chase after spot fires dominate. As a result, such organizations are ill prepared for the rapid emergence of stronger environmental regulations, price rises due to dwindling natural resources supplies, bottlenecks in supply chains due to changes in energy policy, or upsurges in insurance costs due to the rise in damages from extreme weather events.

Normalizing encounters that test our ethical capacities does not mean creating a 'doom and gloom' culture of expecting the worst. Core values are principles that we want to express and use in all the work we do. It is rewarding and enlivening to have a sense of efficacy and autonomy in the values we live by. In contrast, the silencing of our values and the assumption that things cannot be changed is a recipe for reduced enjoyment of life. Normalizing values issues means recognizing the ongoing, ubiquitous need for freely voicing our interests and concerns and that is a life-affirming opportunity for real growth. In a sustainability context, the normalizing of regenerative values is an important social and business goal in the sense that building up and restoring the living systems of the planet should be a default position for many, if not all business. It should not be the rare province of the few. The movement toward regenerativity needs to be normalized if viable and sustainable futures are to be achieved.

Purpose (understanding your personal and professional purposes)

The fourth pillar in GVV is Purpose. This pillar emphasizes the inquiry into what we and our organizations want to achieve, what impact we want to have on others, and who we want to become. Purpose is the process of developing our goals and vision, be they big or small, long-term, or near-term, personal, professional, or organizational. Defining our purpose in a narrow sense is fine, but it is also important to think of purpose broadly because this sets up a moral compass for navigating moral challenges at a more general level. Reflecting on purpose helps to concretize our values, see where they are relevant and how they can be useful for discovering possibilities. Such reflections help to prioritize the goals and ends we work toward and the means we use to get there.

The relationship between goals and means is a crucial one in business as it is in ethics. Ethical theories can be usefully categorized according to whether they emphasis one or other of these perspectives. Code-based theories (deontological theories) pay close attention to the means, to the codes, laws, regulations, commandments, precepts, and industry standards that guide how goals are reached. In contrast, goal-based theories (consequentialist theories) focus on outcomes, the consequences of policies, strategies, and practices on different stakeholders. Theories that discuss ethics as social agreements (social contract theories) aim to include both overarching goals and pragmatic means into an integrative perspective that accommodates both means and ends. Similarly, in business, companies can have varying emphases on their mission/vision, that is, their central purpose, and on the means they use to get there. In fact, the conventional notion of a business model is a formal detailing of the value proposition of a business (the ends) and how it will create that value (the means). For a conventional business, financial profits are the core purpose, and the business models sets out the means for achieving those profits. As we will see in the following pages, regenerative businesses challenge these conventional understanding of means and ends. But this does not mean that profit is left out of the picture. In her book detailing the GVV approach, Gentile quotes the management thinker Charles Handy who asks, "What's a business for?" Hardy answers, "The purpose of business is not to make a profit, full stop. It is to make a profit so that the business can do something more or better." The profit motive is not being left behind here; rather, it is shifted from being the goal to being a means. It is a false dichotomy to ask whether an organization should focus on profits or sustainability. Handy and Gentile are pointing out here that, not only can businesses do both, but that they do so with their purpose being to benefit people and the natural systems they depend on and with money as their means for achieving those goals.

It is not only for-profit organizations that struggle with these prior-itizations. NGOs and social businesses also need to operate and achieve their purpose while maintaining a sound financial footing. The case that we explore using this lens of Purpose is the Swedish international development organization IM and its social business enterprise Humanium Metal. The case highlights the creative ways in which personal and professional pur-poses are balanced with financial responsibilities and opportunities.

Self-knowledge, self-image & alignment

The fifth pillar of Self-knowledge, Self-image and Alignment[2] is about tailoring the manner and objectives for expressing values to your own preferences, skills, and talents. This is so for both personal and organizational contexts. GVV is not about being a hero, having excellent oratory skills or being an extrovert. It is also not about teaching or even persuading people to be more ethical. It assumes that we are already moral creatures who want to express our values and that we can improve in how we do that. GVV is concerned with devel-oping one's personal skill set for holding values-based conversations and activities to achieve a shared purpose. To develop such skills, it is necessary to grow in self-knowledge and self-efficacy and to build on "the strengths and preferences that you already recognize in yourself" (Gentile, 2010a, p. 108). Hence, an important aspect of this pillar of *Self-story* is that there are many ways to voice and enact our values and depending on who we are, our preferences and strengths, we can frame the challenge in a way that plays to *our own strengths* rather than feeling we need to become a different sort of person with skills or personality that we don't have in order to act on our values.

The sets of skills outlined at the beginning of this chapter included technical, financial, coordinating but also social skills in which we included intra-personal competencies such as self-knowledge and self-awareness. Expressing core values in a pragmatic way requires the development of internal capacities of insight and awareness. This is an ongoing process of growth and maturation that might involve, for example, coaching, mentoring, and self-development. To reach objectively measurable sustainability goals, such as the United Nations Sustainable Development Goals (SDGs), it can be assumed that this will mostly involve technical and financial skills but, increasingly, we know these are not enough. For example, the recent emergence of the Inner Development Goals (IDGs) (Ekskäret Foundation, The New Division, & 29k Foundation, 2021) shows the importance of intrapersonal skills in normative processes like sustainability transitions. The IDGs (see Table 2.1) include such skills as developing an inner moral compass, identification, and commitment to one's core values, having an authentic self-image and ability to self-regulate, and having a sense of connectedness to nature and to others. It is no coincidence that the IDGs contain a mixture of subjective (Being, Thinking), objective (Collaborating, Acting), and relational competencies (Relating, Caring). The interaction between Self and Other through Relatedness is where ethics is either supported or stymied.

The GVV pillar of *Self-story* includes these kinds of Self–Other concerns. The more we practice values-based conversations and voicing our values to others, the more competent we become in navigating the complexities and ambiguities of transformative change. Again, this is not about becoming a superhero or "sustainability champion". The emphasis here is on strengthening our self-knowledge, growing our sense of who we are at our best and developing skills that help us establish that ambition. It is also interesting to

Table 2.1 The Inner Development Goals (IDGs)

1. Being — Relationship to self and cultivating our inner life • Inner compass: Feeling a sense of responsibility and commitment to values and purposes. • Integrity and Authenticity: Acting with sincerity, honesty, and integrity. • Learning mindset: Having a basic mindset of curiosity and openness to change. • Self-awareness: Reflecting on one's inner life and self-image. • Presence: Ability to be in the here and now without judgement.
2. Thinking — Cognitive skills • Critical thinking: Skills in critically reviewing evidence and viewpoints. • Complexity awareness: Thinking that can hold ambiguity, complexity, and systems. • Perspective skills: Making use of insights from contrasting perspectives. • Sense-making: Recognizing patterns and creating stories. • Long-term orientation and visioning: Sustaining commitment to integrative visions.
3. Relating — Caring for others and the world • Appreciation: Relating to others and to the world with a basic sense of gratitude and joy. • Connectedness: Feeling connected to a larger whole, with a social-ecological community. • Humility: Act in accordance with the needs of the situation. • Compassion: Relating to others, oneself, and Nature with kindness.
4. Collaborating — Social skills • Communication skills: Listening to others, advocating your own views skilfully. • Co-creation skills: Developing collaborative relationships with diverse stakeholders. • Inclusive mindset: Embracing diversity. • Trust: Show trust by creating and maintaining trusting relationships. • Mobilization skills: Inspiring and mobilizing others to engage in shared purposes.
5. Acting for change — Leading and acting • Self-efficacy: Expressing values and taking relevant action. • Creativity: Generating and developing original ideas, activities, methods, objects. • Optimism: Communicating a sense of confidence. • Perseverance: Remaining engaged and determined.

take an organizational perspective on these qualities. Businesses also need to be sensitive to their own internal organizational climates, their own cultural identity. Businesses are powerful social entities that can choose to be agents of change, to collaborate with stakeholders, to display care and regard for others, or to be present to the needs of its members (or not). The individual notions of *Self-knowledge* and *Self-story* are closely related to the organizational concepts of brand image, organizational identity, and corporate reputation. In the same way that people need to nurture their inner lives and subjective capacities for reflection, organizations also function best when they care for and spend time on developing their own internal climates and cultures. It is only when these alignments take place that organizations can honestly communicate their values through their public image and reputation.

The GVV concept of values alignment is a crucial element here in that people's values systems are always interacting with their aspirations for the future and with their organization's own current and espoused values. The alignments and misalignments between individual and collective values, as expressed currently or aspired to, motivate the consolidation of shared purpose, or alternatively can create conflict and discord. Figure 2.2 depicts these patterns of (mis)alignment for both personal and organizational levels. Personal values are those which individuals currently hold, and their aspirational values are their visions and dreams. Shared values are those that organizations currently hold, and their espoused values are those that they aim to better embody in the future.

Integrity gaps emerge for an individual when there are misalignments between who the person is now and who they intend to be, or when there are discordances between the values they express at work and those they

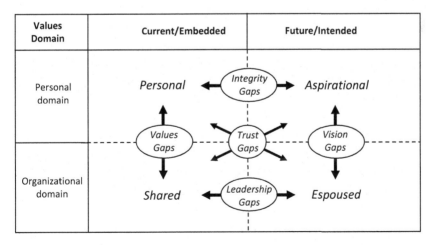

Figure 2.2 Current and future values for the personal and organizational levels.

display at home. When there are misalignments in integrity, people can be overly influenced by social pressure to conform and by situational factors that override their personal values. Tobacco executives, for example, can be law-abiding citizens at home and happily go to work for an industry that harms its customers in vast numbers. This kind of compartmentalization (Rozuel, 2011) of values is a common threat to the building of an ethical organization. Values gaps exist when there are misalignments between the values of the members and those of the organization. This can run both ways. The values of members can be quite different to those of their organizations and the misalignments of these values can lead to the sabotaging of organizational culture or alternatively to the corruption of individual's actions. Visions gaps refer to the disparities between the future goals and purposes of organizational members and the enterprise. Leadership gaps emerge when espoused values of the organization are not realized. All these misalignments disrupt the sense of trust and commitment between the micro/individual, meso/group, and macro/system domains. Trust is created when there is close alignment between the current and espoused values, whether that be for the organization or its members. With trust comes an organizational culture that encourages employee voice and the healthy expression of values, ideas, innovations, concerns, and hopes.

Gaps can also be interpreted as focal points for action and improvement. Figure 2.2 can be regarded as a means for identifying opportunities for values investment and for developing and evaluating key values indicators (KVIs). In entrepreneurial ventures embedding values at the beginning of the project in both personal and organizational domains means that functions such as recruitment and seeking investments can be performed with greater understanding between key parties. There are as many solutions for closing these gaps as there are diverse ways to address workplace challenges. This is one reason ethics can be a powerful source of innovation and motivation. It does not matter if we are risk-averse or risk-takers, extroverts or introverts, skilled speakers or behind-the-scenes operators, we can each develop our own means for creatively resolving problems and grasping opportunities.

It might be assumed that entrepreneurs who follow their purpose and work with regenerative sustainability are all risk-takers who dare to leave the contemporary business world to pursue a risky business career. But this is not true. As we show in the following case stories, regenerative entrepreneurs can also be conservative people interested in retaining what is known and useful, while also aiming to create something new. Hopefully, these stories of regeneration will be sources of inspiration, confidence, and guidance for anyone seeking effective ways to retain what we know to be good and useful while ushering in transformative change.

Voice (acting on your values)

The sixth pillar of *Voice* proposes that the practice of expressing values helps to build ethical competencies over time. *Voice* here should be understood as a metaphor for any personal activity or organizational practice of expressing core values. While the idea of *expressing* values can be typically thought of as speaking up, writing down, or articulating our concerns in some way, it does not necessarily need to involve proactive behavior. *Voice* can be just as well expressed through listening to and for the values of others. At the organizational level, *Voice* can be expressed through the creation of psychologically safe and supportive environments where others feel they can speak out their feelings and thoughts. For example, a CEO's attempt to build a culture of *Voice* in her organization might include the practice of listening for and inviting a greater diversity of voices to be heard in boardroom meetings. Especially for the formal leadership roles in a business, *Voice* is as much about listening as it is about expressing. Gentile has emphasized that GVV can assist senior leadership to "create and maintain an organizational culture that encourages and enables and supports voicing values", and a powerful way to do this is by creating workplaces where people are listened to, and their values are heard. As Gentile says,

> If and when employees do raise values-related questions, the manner in which their manager receives the message sends powerful signals about whether this sort of behavior is genuinely welcome.
>
> (Gentile, 2016, p. 110)

Voice has been a very visible aspect of the sustainability movement in recent years with the appearance of young people like Greta Thunberg[3] and the many millions of young people who have marched, organized, or initiated other actions such as legal proceedings. It has also been a powerful dimension of the movement toward new kinds of business organizations that place social and ecological benefits on at least an equal footing with economic outcomes. The emergence of new forms of ownership, B-Corp Certification, and social innovation enterprises all demonstrate the innovation in business that is expressing dissatisfaction with mainstream economic and consumerist values and the desire to do things differently. In the cases that follow this move toward expressing distinct kinds of values through organizational innovation goes many steps further than mere discontent. The voicing of regenerative values completely flips the standard capitalist priorities of profitability, efficiency, and functionality to regard them as means for achieving social and ecological ends. Many voices will need to be raised and listened to if the rapid emergence of regenerative businesses is to come about.

Rationalizations (overcoming inhibiting arguments and developing enabling responses)

The heart of GVV pedagogy and theory lies in holding conversations that enable ethical opportunities. It is in conversation, the activity of people communicating with each other, where the GVV rubber hits the road of ethical improvement. Conversations between stakeholders are the foundation of any organizational purpose, process, or function. There are some crucial elements in values-based conversations that GVV draws special attention to. The pivotal element is *Rationalizations*. A rationalization is a reason or argument that silences or mutes the expression of a core value. Rationalizations can be targeted toward individuals. For example, "You should not speak up about this issue because it is not your responsibility". Rationalizations can also be targeted toward a more general audience. For example, it is frequently argued that the purpose of business is to create wealth and to provide employment. Any additional goal, it is argued, will divert money away from these core activities and so less wealth and fewer jobs will be created. According to this reasoning, sustainability should not be a priority if it comes at the cost of economic growth and employment. Such arguments act to mute or silence environmental values and social values of equity and justice. The "jobs and growth" mantra is often proffered to demonstrate the illogical nature of calls for sustainability and to move the responsibility for attending to such values to governments instead of businesses. The values that might be associated with sustainability such as respect for nature, compassion for traditional owners, responsibility to future generations, or honest presentation of the relevant science are rendered secondary or even silenced by claims that it will create unemployment and less economic wealth for investors and shareholders who bear the financial risks.

The "jobs and growth" mantra is a rationalization because it silences core values. It just so happens that this common objective to sustainability regulations and imperatives is also highly debatable. There is a substantial body of research that shows that businesses that have better sustainability or environmental, social and governance (ESG) evaluations are more profitable over the long term. Putting the empirical realities aside, the process of rationalization, of presenting reasons to silence core values, creates conditions that systematically support unethical activity. First, embedded forms of rationalization serve to silence people from speaking up. When an organizational culture routinely censors important conversations, for example, on sustainability transitioning, many other topics get silenced as well. A toxic culture of command-and-control leadership often ensues. Second, in silencing values, the rationalization process also silences innovation and the capacity of people to suggest new ideas. Rationalizations tend to favor retention of the status quo, and this underestimates members' capacity for undertaking transformative change and for resolving conflicting demands or ambiguous tensions. Many organizations perform well financially while prioritizing social and environmental goals. It is a false dichotomy to place "jobs and growth" in opposition to sustainability investment and to assume the only choice we have is for Business-As-Usual. Rationalizations are often employed to defend the perpetuation of false dichotomies and to close down conversations about change. Third, rationalizations generate cultures of silence that promote harassment and discrimination. When people see that voicing their values gets met with management disapproval, ostracization, or other subtle forms of psychological punishment, all manner of concerns get silenced, and the possibility of toxic and even abusive cultures emerges. At its heart, a culture of rationalization develops when those in positions of power attempt to quash views they see as threatening. This is why systematic rationalization serves to disempower workers and organizational members with no formal power base. Fourth, rationalizations are dehumanizing in that they externalize the responsibility for the social and environmental impact of businesses onto other players – including governments, local communities, activists, and vulnerable communities.

In the process of building and maintaining a regenerative organization, values-based challenges frequently emerge because the goal of regenerativity continuously rubs up against the priorities of mainstream profit-focused market capitalism. When entrepreneurs choose to work regeneratively, they encounter many arguments, both internally from themselves and externally from others, that reason against following their alternative pathway. What helps regenerative entrepreneurs to counter such propositions? How do regenerative entrepreneurs anticipate and prepare for the rationalizing arguments they will most likely face? We hope to address these and other questions and find out how these business leaders manage to create such radically transformative organizations.

Pairing GVV pillars with our regenerative business cases

Gentile says that, taken together, the 7 pillars are "a kind of action framework or 'to-do list' for voicing our values" (Gentile, 2010a) and there is a systematic action logic to how they complement and build on each other. The logic might be described as follows: 1) Values: Possessing a set of core values (derived from a multitude of individual experiences and social sources) guides the expression of our ethical commitments. 2) Choice: Our choices function to either strengthen our capacity to enact those values or not. 3) Normalization: Because choice is built into (but not necessarily exercised) the everyday act of decision-making, ethical actions and choice are normal aspects of the workplace. 4) Purpose: The expression (or silencing) of values-based choices impacts on our sense of purpose and on how we think of ourselves. 5) Self-knowledge and Self-image: The personal history of how we express (or not) our core commitments shapes our personal identity and self-image. 6) Voice: Our personal history of ethical actions and identity informs not only whether we voice our values or not but also how skilfully we do that. 7) Rationalizations: How we practically respond to rationalizations and neutralizations that can disengage us from our moral identity and core values is key to developing our competencies for creatively disclosing and expressing our values.

From this logic the GVV Pillars can be regarded as a performative cycle that moves from awareness of values to self-identity to action and expression and back to core values. Some authors have presented this cycle as a process of moral awareness, judgement, motivation, and action (Hannah, Avolio, & May, 2011; Rest, 1986). GVV pedagogy emphasizes the importance of entering this cycle from the point of action and expression of values. Through performative practice of those skills involved in expressing our core values we become more aware of what our values are and their everyday relevance to the work we do. The following describes which pillars we pair with our illustrative cases and the rationales for doing so.

Chapter 3: Values and Choice – Earth Regenerators: Values and choice lie at the heart of Earth Regenerators approach to regenerative sustainability. We pair choice and values because together they make the possible real. Values guide the movement toward a purpose or vision and choice acts to motivate the selection of pathways based on that guidance. Earth Regenerators (ER) is a community organization that embodies regenerative values in a radical way. Based on the latest science, ER entrepreneurs see economic collapse as unavoidable; nevertheless, regenerative choices are still available for post-collapse communities. Realizing that we can still express our values creates the possibilities we need to choose between.

Chapter 4: Normalizing the Voicing of Values – Commonland: Commonland is a regenerative organization supporting farmers and agricultural communities to make regeneration one of the default choices for sustainable investments. The entrepreneurs in this case are keenly aware of that the standard agricultural practices are causing environmental and social problems on a global scale. These unsustainable practices are the accepted standard in many farming regions. Commonland entrepreneurs are constantly challenging these prevailing practices and challenging communities to review what they regard as normal and acceptable in the farming communities that generate primary produce.

Chapter 5: Self-Story and Purpose – Humanium Metal: We focus here on the interplay between self-story, self-knowledge, and personal and organizational alignments in the social business Humanium Metal (HM). The entrepreneurs in this case discuss aspects of their personal journeys and how these autobiographic elements feed into their professional purpose and align with the organizational mission of HM.

Chapter 6: Rationalizations and Voice – The Seaweed Company: In this chapter we delve into the topic of rationalizations and how these processes of disengaging from moral responsibility interact with individual and collective capacity for voicing concerns, visions, and innovations. The company often needs to deal with inhibiting arguments for building up its business and voicing its regenerative mission in conventional markets.

Chapter 7: Integrating all 7 Pillars – Insights and Implications: In this chapter we pull all the insights from the other chapters together and see how regenerativity values are voiced to create deep sustainability transitions and transformative business strategies.

GVV and regenerative sustainability

In exploring our illustrative cases through the various GVV lenses we aim to disclose some of the micro-foundational dynamics of regenerative transformations in organizational contexts. GVV is an action-based approach to business ethics, and it places communicative activities and interactions at the center of all the challenges and opportunities that sustainability transitions present. We hope the cases and the insights derived from them will be instructive and inspirational to others in understanding the factors involved in developing regenerative voices for supporting deep sustainability transitions in all types of organizations.

Notes

1 See, for example, Habermas's discourse ethics (1984), Bird's moral muteness theory of Bird (1996), Lévinas' ethic of reciprocity (1985), Honneth's social recognition theory (2014) and Hirschman's theory of employee voice (1970).

2 With Gentile, we also refer to this pillar as "*Self-story*" because an individual's personal life narrative includes their self-knowledge and self-image in a coherent story of who they are.

3 For example, Alexandria Villaseñor (United States of America), Luisa Neubauer (Germany), Autumn Peltier (Canada), and Ridhima Pandey (India).

References

Arce, D. G., & Gentile, M. C. (2014). Giving voice to values as a leverage point in business ethics education. *Journal of Business Ethics, 131*(3), 535–542. doi:10.1007/s10551-014-2470-7

Austin, J. L. (1975). *How to Do Things with Words*. Oxford: Oxford University Press.

Bird, F. (1996). *The Muted Conscience: Moral Silence and the Practice of Ethics in Business*. Westport, CT: Quorum Books.

Blok, V. (2013). The power of speech acts: Reflections on a performative concept of ethical oaths in economics and business. *Review of Social Economy, 71*(2), 187–208. doi:10.1080/00346764.2013.799965

Donaldson, T., & Dunfee, T. W. (1994). Toward a unified conception of business ethics: Integrated social contracts theory. *Academy of Management Review, 19*(2), 252–284.

Dyllick, T., & Muff, K. (2016). Clarifying the meaning of sustainable business: Introducing a typology from business-as-usual to true business sustainability. *Organization & Environment, 29*(2), 156–174. doi:10.1177/10860 26615575176

Edwards, M. G., & Kirkham, N. (2014). Situating 'Giving Voice to Values': A metatheoretical evaluation of a new approach to business ethics. *Journal of Business Ethics, 121*(3), 477–495. doi:10.1007/s10551-013-1738-7

Ekskäret Foundation, The New Division, & 29k Foundation. (2021). *Inner Development Goals*. Retrieved from https://www.innerdevelopmentgoals. org/

Gentile, M. C. (2010a). *Giving Voice to Values: How to Speak Your Mind When You Know What's Right*. New Haven, CT: Yale University Press.

Gentile, M. C. (2010b). Managing yourself: Keeping your colleagues honest. *Harvard Business Review, 88*(3).

Gentile, M. C. (2016). Listening for values. *Humanistic Management Journal, 1*, 107–111.

Gentile, M. C. (2017). Giving voice to values: A pedagogy for behavioral ethics. *Journal of Management Education, 41*(4), 469–479.

Habermas, J. (1984). *The Theory of Communicative Action* (Vol. 1). Boston, MA: McCarthy.

Hannah, S. T., Avolio, B. J., & May, D. R. (2011). Moral maturation and moral conation: A capacity approach to explaining moral thought and action. *Academy of Management Review, 36*(4), 663–685.

Hirschman, A. O. (1970). *Exit, Voice, and Loyalty: Responses to Decline in Firms, Organizations, and States*. Harvard: Harvard University Press.

Honneth, A. (2014). The normativity of ethical life. In I. Testa, L. Ruggiu, & L. Cortella (Eds.), *I That Is We, We That Is I. Perspectives on Contemporary Hegel: Social Ontology, Recognition, Naturalism, and the Critique of Kantian Constructivism* (pp. 157–168). Leiden: Brill.

Jones, D. R., Visser, M., Stokes, P., Örtenblad, A., Deem, R., Rodgers, P., & Tarba, S. Y. (2020). The performative university: 'Targets', 'Terror' and 'Taking Back Freedom' in academia. *Management Learning, 51*(4), 363–377. doi:10.1177/1350507620927554

Labuschagne, C., Brent, A. C., & van Erck, R. P. G. (2005). Assessing the sustainability performances of industries. *Journal of Cleaner Production, 13*(4), 373–385. doi:10.1016/j.jclepro.2003.10.007

Lévinas, E. (1985). *Ethics and Infinity: Conversations with Philippe Nemo*. Livonia, MI: Duquesne University Press.

Mies, A., & Gold, S. (2021). Mapping the social dimension of the circular economy. *Journal of Cleaner Production, 321*, 128960. doi:10.1016/j.jclepro.2021.128960

Miller, W. F., & Shawver, T. J. (2021). Giving voice to values: Operationalizing ethical decision-making in accounting. In M. Pinheiro & A. Costa (Eds.), *Accounting Ethics Education: Making Ethics Real* (pp. 131–157). London: Routledge.

Poponi, S., Colantoni, A., Cividino, S. R. S., & Mosconi, E. M. (2019). The stakeholders' perspective within the B Corp certification for a circular approach. *Sustainability, 11*(6), 1584.

Rest, J. (1986). *Moral Development: Advances in Research and Theory*. New York, NY: Praeger.

Rozuel, C. (2011). The moral threat of compartmentalization: Self, roles and responsibility. *Journal of Business Ethics, 102*(4), 685–697. doi:10.1007/s10551-011-0839-4

Sagiv, L., Roccas, S., Cieciuch, J., & Schwartz, S. H. (2017). Personal values in human life. *Nature Human Behaviour, 1*(9), 630–639. doi:10.1038/s41562-017-0185-3

Schwartz, S. H., & Bardi, A. (2001). Value hierarchies across cultures: Taking a similarities perspective. *Journal of Cross-Cultural Psychology, 32*(3), 268–290. doi:10.1177/0022022101032003002

Shawver, T. J., & Miller, W. F. (2021). Assessing the impact of values change using giving voice to values. In C. R. Baker (Ed.), *Research on Professional Responsibility and Ethics in Accounting* (Vol. 24, pp. 1–18). Emerald Publishing Limited.

3

VALUES AND CHOICE IN EARTH REGENERATION

This chapter examines the role values play in the process of choosing who we desire to be and how we seek to build and maintain regenerative organizations. We tell the story of *Earth Regenerators* (ER) and the *Design School for Regenerating Earth* and two entrepreneurs engaged in the development of these global community and membership-based organizations as they experiment and discover ways to live and design their personal and professional lives within a "collapse aware" community. Our entrepreneurs, Joe Brewer and JP Parker, explain how significant it has been for them to question the status quo and to engage with their community in regenerative entrepreneurial activity. We cover concepts and topics such as pro-social behavior, developmental entrenchment, the paradox of choice, an extended sense of responsibility and collapse awareness.

DOI: 10.4324/9781003330660-3

THE CASE OF *EARTH REGENERATORS* AND THE *DESIGN SCHOOL FOR REGENERATING EARTH* IN BRIEF

Organization name: Earth Regenerators

Year of founding: Earth Regenerators 2020; Design School for Regenerating Earth 2022

Type of organization: Online and onsite community organization

Purpose: Earth Regenerators and the Design School for Regenerating Earth are online and onsite organizations for people who want to participate in discussion and education groups for designing regenerative communities and pursuing regenerative projects.

Industry/community sector: Community education

Products or services: Online and onsite facilities and events are offered that support regenerative learning and practices and opportunities for practical projects.

- Online offerings include: podcasts, learning journeys, regenerative project incubator
- Onsite projects include: Barichara Regeneration Fund, Eco-regeneration and community in Costa Rica, The Culture Centre on the Earth Regenerators Mighty Networks

Location, major stakeholders and size: Originally founded by Joe Brewer in Barichara, Colombia, ER and the Design School for Regenerating Earth, now offer online courses and support for onsite communities in countries across the world.

Impact and achievements: Over 4,000 online community participants, offering dozens of online activities every month, including study groups, bioregional learning sessions, community discussion spaces, opportunities for designing and running rituals and ceremonies, and food and nutrition circles.

Websites: Earth Regenerators https://earth-regenerators.mn.co/

Design School for Regenerating Earth: https://design-school-for-regenerating-earth.mn.co/

What choice do we have?

A major obstacle to voicing one's core concerns or dreams of possibility is the assumption that things cannot be changed, that no alternative exists or that, if some option did exist, it would be impossible to realize. Believing that we have no choice or that some prevailing social system is permanent robs us of exercising the most fundamental of all ethical qualities – the capacity to choose. If no choice exists, there can be no motive for action. Several thinkers (including Fredrik Jameson, Slavoj Žižek, and Mark Fisher) have proposed that one of the most problematic features of the current economic order, the system of free-market capitalism that dominates environmental, social, and economic realities, is that it appears to be naturally pre-given, ubiquitously present, and, therefore, practically unchangeable. As Mark Fisher puts it, there appears to be a "widespread sense that not only is capitalism the only viable political and economic system, but also that it is now impossible even to imagine a coherent alternative to it" (Fisher, 2009, p. 2). In the face of such assumptions, we have no choice, no freedom to propose something new and innovative.

The problem is that there are some core structural features and practices of the current economic system that are driving global ecologies toward greater instability, lower resilience, and into degraded and destabilized ecological states which, in turn, have immense social impacts. Should we not choose to do things differently? If the current economic system is driving climate change and biodiversity collapse, it is rational to imagine different economic pathways and choose alternatives that realistically offer the possibility for building flourishing ecologies and resilient social communities. If current systems are burdening future generations with damaging levels of financial debt and environmental pollution, then perhaps fresh design pathways for organizing future communities should be explored. These possibilities will not occur without choosing to question current assumptions, generate feasible alternatives, and deliberate on the choices to be made.

One of the most important functions of the regenerative entrepreneur is to pragmatically challenge this assumption of no choice at the big scale. To challenge the deterministic view that there is no possibility of transforming the current status quo of the global system that is causing such environmental damage. One distinctive feature of the regenerative entrepreneur that separates them from more conventional entrepreneuring is this systems-level scale of new thinking. The real impact of a regenerative business is only recognized when seen in the context of systemic economic transformation. This does not mean that the enterprise must *operate* on the global scale. It does mean that the full purpose of regenerativity comes to the fore when the background of systemic change is added to the picture.

Regenerative entrepreneurs choose to create and manage their organizations with this background of systemic change in mind.

Regenerative entrepreneurs demonstrate, through their actions, that choice is possible, and that values and personal virtues exist which can guide the proactive creation of viable choices. Once the possibility of choice has been established, values act to not only imagine what worlds might be created, but what worlds are plausible and possible. Entrepreneurs are business-people who generate possibilities, and they interrogate those possibilities to find the ones that are plausible, realizable, and useful. The art of entrepreneurial innovation is the meeting of imaginative choice and possibility with pragmatic value and action. The GVV pillars of *Choice* and *Value* are eminently useful partners to explore the creative world of our case for this chapter – *Earth Regenerators* and the *Design School for Regenerating Earth*.

Regenerative entrepreneurs and the extractive economy

One way to describe the ideas of regenerativity is to contrast it with the notion of an extractive business or economy. To understand the genesis of the organizations presented in this chapter we will further explore this contrast and discuss the notion of an extractive economy. In Chapter 1 we saw that regenerativity comes in different forms – economic, social, and environmental – and that Kate Raworth's Doughnut Economics is a way of thinking about the relationship between all three. The Doughnut model posits that sustainability is a place of balance between respecting environmental boundaries while also meeting the socio-economic needs of communities. Accordingly, Raworth distinguishes between regenerative businesses, which achieve this balance, and extractive businesses, which do not. We might make the same distinction between regenerative and extractive entrepreneurs. The extractive entrepreneur asks how to maximize the extraction of financial values from this new enterprise irrespective of the impact of this project of environmental or social limits. In contrast, the regenerative entrepreneur asks how to maximize the benefits produced by a company for its financial, social, and ecological stakeholders. To achieve its purpose of extracting maximum profit, the extractive enterprise seeks to externalize as many costs as legally (and sometimes illegally) possible, including those to ecological and social systems.

The regenerative pathway is to externalize the creation of shared value. The goal with regenerativity is not to siphon off one form of value at the cost of other forms but to generate as many forms of value as possible. For example, extractive business models favor linear cradle-to-grave approaches because under this take–make–use–waste model a great many costs and responsibilities can be externalized. The linear model allows a business to externalize the social and environmental costs of extracting materials from the Earth, their transformation into products, and the costs that accrue after the point of sale to the customer. In other words, linearity allows non-responsibility. Linear business models are useful for businesses that aim to minimize economic, social, and environmental liabilities. In contrast, business models that favor circularity aim to maintain and re-establish relationships throughout the life cycle of a product so that benefits are created for as many stakeholders as possible. This is the circular or cradle-to-cradle approach of the regenerative economy. Circular regenerative models aim to connect economic, social, and environmental values rather than separate them so that some can be internalized/owned and others externalized/disowned. Using Raworth's metaphor, the move from extractive to regenerative business is, at the very least, the transformation of the linear "caterpillar economy" to the circular "butterfly economy".

However, this movement toward a regenerative and circular economy will require much more than niche 'green' businesses to adopt circularity practices in their production of goods and services. A circular economy requires extensive cooperation between businesses, governments, and communities. Among many profound shifts, circularity requires governments to change regulations and taxation laws, banks and reinsurers to respond to the risks of financing linear economy businesses, international networks of shareholders to require their corporations to address ongoing issues of pollution and waste, citizens to support policies that radically change economic infrastructures, and consumers to move toward more informed choices in what they purchase. In other words, circularity, at the scale needed to address global environmental problems, requires extensive economic transformation on a global scale. Every sector of the community will have a role to play and while many players in the old economy will need to be superseded, the opportunities for regenerative, circular, and more collaborative forms of generating value will also be global in scale.

How might this new economy emerge and what will it look like? This is the space of creative experimentation that Earth Regenerators occupies.

The case – Earth Regenerators[1]

In the case of Earth Regenerators, we peer into the world of possibilities that lies beyond extractive capitalism, to where regenerative and circular economies and communities are beginning to emerge. To help us do that we employ the Giving Voice to Values lenses of *Choice* and *Values*. These pillars are particularly relevant here because shifting large systems or moving beyond them requires the deliberate exercising of choice and a deep change in how values are applied. To influence and transform large systems requires the recognition that viable choices do exist, that they can be imagined, and that we are equipped with values that can inform and realize those possibilities. In the following we tell the story of how the regenerative entrepreneurs Joe Brewer, JP Parker, and the innovative community of Earth Regenerators are questioning the status quo and creating regenerative design pathways toward what they see as healthy forms of economy and society. They are establishing a global entrepreneurial community that recognizes it does have a choice to do things differently.

Earth Regenerators (ER) is a world-wide network of communities aiming to facilitate the emergence of truly regenerative economies and societies. ER started up in early 2020 with a small online discussion group and now comprises of more than 4000 participants. ER takes a radical perspective on sustainability because they see the science as demanding that kind of response. Sustainability-as-usual for them is not an option. From the ER perspective, the latest scientific research clearly warns that catastrophic change is likely in the coming decades and that no process of incremental intervention will significantly shift that trajectory. The Covid-19 pandemic, the global water and energy crises, the Central American climate refugees, the world-wide demise of coral reefs, the degradation of the Earth's cryosphere (as evidenced in the runaway melting of the Greenland ice shelf), the East African famine, alterations in oceanic chemistry and currents, all these and many other large-scale environmental problems are regional evidence for what Earth system scientists have been warning of for several decades – the possibility of global biophysical collapse (Bradshaw et al., 2021; Butzer, 2012; Willcock, Cooper, Addy, & Dearing, 2023).

What is interesting about ER is that they choose to take a (re)construc-tive view toward this possibility of collapse. They look at these warnings and choose to respond creatively by designing programs and activities that restore the biosphere on multiple fronts: education, community building, social innovation, and environmental activism. Founder Joe Brewer states in his recent book, *The Design Pathway for Regenerating Earth*, that that the ER com-munity works to embrace "the fundamental insight that all living systems self-organize around the patterns of regeneration" (Brewer, 2021). He goes on to say that:

> Applied to the scale of entire landscapes, this [self-organization] reveals how all truly sustainable human cultures throughout history were organized at the territorial scale as bioregional economies. A planet-wide network of learning ecosystems is needed that can hold the complexity of birthing these regenerative bioregions during and after the rest of the collapse that we were all born into.
>
> (Brewer, 2021)

From humble online group origins, the ER has grown to become an estab-lished player in the field of regenerative sustainability. ER exists as both face-to-face and online communities and so encapsulates the local and global aspects of sustainability transitions in direct ways. The organiza-tion offers online educational programs, called learning journeys, such as "Regenerative Finance" to explore what regenerative economics is and how to apply it in everyday life, "Regenerative Conversations" to learn how to establish bio-regional landscapes and ecological restoration projects, and "Prosocial groups for Earth Regeneration" to learn how to create effective and harmonious groups in service of life on Earth. It also includes specific projects in local areas. For example, an ER project incubator has developed where the members help each other with start-ups, community projects, and neighborhood activities by organizing advisory circles, design thinking processes, collaborating to create regenerative projects, as well as co-creat-ing various curriculums for regenerating earth.

As an online community, ER members come from places across the world. They want to learn about alternative communities and to be involved in regen-erative development and educational projects. ER taps into a global market of people who are unhappy with the materialistic direction of society, busi-ness, and the economy and with the negative impacts of economic activity on human communities and natural systems. The rapid development of ER as an organization comes out of this widespread need for a more ecologically grounded way of life. But it took the entrepreneurial instincts of its founders and original organizers, and especially to the work of the regenerative entrepreneurs Joe Brewer and JP Parker, to harness those motivations and provide a space and opportunity for the ER community to emerge.

The entrepreneurs

Joe Brewer – Founder and co-facilitator

Joe Brewer is the founder of Earth Regenerators (ER). For more than 20 years, he has worked to find viable means for shifting public thinking about global systems of economy, education, commerce, and agriculture toward more sustainable futures. He has previously initiated similar initiatives to bring people together from diverse backgrounds with the same purpose of transitioning communities into more sustainable ways of living and making livelihoods. Informed by his close reading of the latest environmental and Earth system science, Joe has embarked on an intellectual journey of studying complexity, Earth systems, cognitive science, and cultural evolution. He describes his prior career before founding ER in 2020 as a 20-year-long journey of trying to create a science of large-scale, social change to help humanity guide itself through the grand social and environmental predicaments it faces.

People who start new social ventures often go through an initial phase of critical inquiry, information gathering, and self-reflection. Joe has gone through several such periods of intense self-questioning regarding each of the social innovations with which he has been involved. His personal history and change of lifestyle demonstrate the importance of values, self-reflection, and choice in his own personal story. He questioned living a life that left a heavy ecological footprint well beyond his own share of the planet's carrying capacity. He questioned whether he should have children, what professional role he could play, and even questioned his own personal existence. While many go through these kinds of reflective phases in their lives, for Joe, this questioning initiated a period of active exploration into what he truly valued in his life and what type of person he wanted to be. In 2018, he began to search seriously for a place where he could collaborate with others in building a regenerative community and a truly sustainable life. He moved to Costa Rica for a year and lived in various communities even as he was working online to develop a social network of people who shared similar ideas about choosing to express their values in alternative ways. He had already been involved in several online educational and social change initiatives and had learned how to mobilize individuals and groups to develop online communities. During this time, over a brief period of just a few months, his thoughts and notes crystallized into a series of chapters that eventually became the book, *The Design Pathway for Regenerating the Earth* (Brewer, 2021).

What Joe realized from that period of inquiry was that his knowledge needed to be shared. He wanted to distribute what he had learned to other like-minded individuals. To embody his values Joe and his family chose to live in an unusual way – off the financial grid, in a country with many social conflicts but also many cultural advantages for living close to the land. In 2019 he moved to Barichara, a small, picturesque town of around 5,000 inhabitants in the northeast of Colombia in South America. Immediately Joe felt that this was a community he could work both with and for. At the end of 2019 Joe wrote a post on social media, asking people to join a study group about the unpublished manuscript for his book. He had no idea that this study group would grow into a planetary-wide platform for gathering and supporting those seeking to regenerate their little bit of the Earth. Six months after moving there, an online community of over 2,000 people had gathered to study Joe's new book – *The Design Pathway for Regenerating Earth*. This rapid growth demonstrates the interest that many have in regenerative sustainability. From Barichara, Joe contributes to the global development of ER through developing and facilitating educational and developmental courses. The study group has now transformed to an expansive platform where over 4,000 change makers who are studying and working for earth regeneration.

In his own life, Joe is trying to embody the pathway to Earth regeneration, and this close personal identity with the values of the organization plays a distinct role in the creation and continuous building up of ER. He says of his own founder's journey:

> I embody in my life everything that gave birth to Earth Regenerators. There's no possibility of separating myself from the work or from the community. It is a way of living into a future indigenous lifeway for the prospect of human survival during planetary collapse. And so, I would

say my involvement in Earth Regenerators relates to everything from
how I form deep love relationships, to how I raise my child, to how I
choose to spend every moment of my waking life. While not meaning
that I'm obsessed and a workaholic, but rather quite the opposite to
the fullest extent possible, I live regeneratively as a way of *being*, and
then role model that, and scaffold that for others to follow.

JP Parker – Community host and technical organizer

JP Parker is a central figure in the emergence of ER and in its success as a
viable online and onsite community. JP holds a bachelor's degree in philosophy and a master's degree in psychology. She describes herself as a
recovering futurist who lives and works at the intersection of exponential
technology, ecology, and culture. As she says:

I have been on this path my entire life. And that is true for many of us;
I am certainly not alone on Earth Regenerators. We have been looking for our people, our fellows, our tribe. What's unusual about Earth
Regenerators is that there's something on the platform we call being
collapse-aware.

JP has been building online communities since the early 1990s and she
has been a serious student of what makes an online community durable
and enlivening. She says, "I like to know when they succeed, and why they
succeed."

This background helped JP be an important player in the early beginnings
of ER and she has been a key person in building up ER's online platform. She
saw that Joe needed someone to head up the administrative and organizing
work that is crucial, especially for the online aspect of ER's work. Through
her role as community host and technical organizer, JP is involved in most
of the ER initiatives. She has been particularly instrumental in creating one
of the cornerstones of ER philosophy and practice – "prosocial process"
(Atkins, Wilson, & Hayes, 2019). We will further explore this values-based
practice in the following sections, but it is important to note that JP intro-
duced this prosocial ethic at a critical juncture in the ER's initial start-up
phase. It has remained a crucial value for the ER community ever since.

JP has emphasized other ethical constructs that have been important in
ER's growth to this point. Two values-based ideas that have been especially

influential in the emergence of ER's identity are being a 'planetary custodian' and 'collapse awareness'. JP explains the ethical sense of custodianship as being fundamental for achieving lasting sustainability. She says that:

> The answer is not to get on a spaceship and colonize Mars – more colonization is not the answer. Stewardship is the answer and cleaning up the mess that we've made, healing the damage we've done while stopping the machinery that's continuing to extract and destroy is essential.

Collapse awareness is a special characteristic of the ER identity and more will be discussed on this later. Like Joe, JP closely identifies with working in the field of regenerative sustainability. She says that regenerative entrepreneurship no longer feels like a matter of choice; it is now a part of her identity and therefore something that defines who she is and how she contributes to the ER community.

What does the science say?

Sharing viewpoints on sustainability is a useful activity. People can share knowledge and experience and get informed about how to become more sustainable in their own private lives. But what if people took the research findings on the biophysical state of the planet seriously? What if communities and their leaders acted on that knowledge and prepared for the changes that are likely to occur? In other words: are the views of the founders of ER, and of those participating in ER discussions, founded on a reasonable interpretation of the science? It is important to provide some nuance and background to ER's and Joe's strong views on 'transgressing planetary boundaries' and 'societal collapse' to better appreciate their framing of regenerative sustainability. In the introductory chapters, a very brief overview of some of the most recent scientific findings about the state of health of the planet's biophysical conditions was outlined. It does not make for happy reading. There is insufficient room to go into the science that underpins these findings. The interested reader might use the earlier references as a starting point to explore some of this material. But it is useful to note that Joe's book, and many of the resources provided for ER educational and discussion groups, rely heavily on the ideas and findings of the Planetary

Boundaries research program. This widely acclaimed Earth system science research perspective was described earlier but its relevance to this chapter is important because the ER community should not be regarded as a fringe community of 'survivalists' or 'preppers' getting ready for some millennialist doomsday event. The ER worldview is heavily informed by very conventional approaches to scientific research and their approach to regenerativity comes from a close reading of this scientific material. Joe's book, *The Design Pathway for Regenerating the Earth*, is full of scientific information and citations from reputable scientific sources. While their interpretation of this material can be debated, it is important to note that the latest science plays a major role in ER discussions and perspective on regenerativity.

Close familiarity with the science is itself an interesting dimension of ER and this question of responses to the science has many ethical implications. ER engages with the science in a conscious and deliberate fashion that marks them out from most other community environmental and sustainability groups where scientific findings on global systems play a much less significant role. This stance raises important ethical questions about what our moral responses to events like climate change should be.

The role of *Values* and *Choice* in the Earth Regenerators community
Values-based leadership

In their professional and leadership work with ER, both Joe and JP aim to be consistently guided by widely shared core values of honesty, respect, responsibility, fairness, and compassion. The aspiration to embody values like these is not unusual in the fields of social innovation or community development. However, the ER case does highlight two noteworthy aspects of this values-based approach to leadership.

First, these values were applied to guide Joe and JP's professional work and to building up ER as a globally networked organization. These values were not compartmentalized into the private sphere of family life or social life, but were integrated within the world of formal work, business, and organizational life. Values such as compassion were taken as a stimulus for inner work and for internalizing qualities that were regarded as central for ER's development and mission. The word integrity can be usefully applied here. A person has integrity when they act consistently, when they uphold the same ethical standards across social and situation boundaries. A leader with integrity expresses their core values across all domains of life and, in particular, does not leave them behind when they walk through the front door at the workplace. An organization has integrity when it applies its core values without discrimination to all its stakeholders and rightholders. Joe's choice to move himself and his family from one of the richest to one of the poorest counties in the world is an illustration of this integrity. Relocating from the United States to Colombia, and moving off what might be called the 'affluence grid', is a powerful demonstration of a values-based commitment.

A second notable aspect of this value-based style of leadership is that Joe and JP embed these values in their work and in the ER organization to emphasize global and intergenerational timescales. The application of these values across extended circles of stakeholders and rightholders[2] and large-scale spatial and temporal frames is a definitive characteristic of both these entrepreneurs and the ER organization. Regeneration as a fundamental goal of ER can only be achieved over long timeframes and necessarily involves multiple human and non-human stakeholders across many regions of the world. Their implementation of the value of responsibility, for example, reaches across times and places to embrace both human societies and planetary ecologies. They enact these values toward other people, but even more pointedly toward nature herself. They choose not only to critically question the assumptions, goals, and practices of the current socio-economic system, but to establish and design pathways that create, what they see as, more regenerative possibilities for all forms of life.

"Collapse awareness"

One concept that holds special importance in ER's sense of organizational responsibility is being "collapse aware". This term refers to the recognition that human economic activity has exceeded the carrying capacity of the planet to the point where serious shifts in planetary systems are unavoidable. We are living in times when our ecological system is collapsing, and it is up to humanity to work regeneratively to create a landing from this collapse that is as smooth as possible. The term is playing a significant role in both their personal and professional lives. JP Parker explains that the term shifts her view on entrepreneurship and supports why she identifies as a recovering futurist. She says,

> Collapse awareness means we've already understood the degree by which we have exceeded the planetary boundaries. We've already understood how damaged things are and that some form of both ecological and economic collapse are coming. It's a fantasy at this point to say we can still avert it. We can reduce the severity of it, but it's already happening.

As mentioned earlier, 'collapse awareness' is not to be equated with millennialism or apocalyptic systems of belief. ER is not a religious community awaiting the final reckoning. The notion of collapse awareness is based on a reading of the scientific literature that we have passed the point of avoiding severe collapse in several of the planetary processes that maintain a stable Earth system. For example, there is mounting scientific evidence that: i) the Earth has transgressed six of the nine boundaries that define planetary stability and resilience (Persson et al., 2022; Steffen et al., 2015; Wang-Erlandsson et al., 2022), ii) we are entering the sixth great extinction event (Bar-On, Phillips, & Milo, 2018; Ceballos, Ehrlich, & Dirzo, 2017; Cowie, Bouchet, & Fontaine, 2022), iii) that tipping points have been crossed in several crucial biophysical systems (Armstrong McKay et al., 2022; Brovkin et al., 2021; Lenton et al., 2019), and iv) that devastating climate change is now unavoidable (IPCC et al., 2022). Admitting to the science that supports these possibilities is regarded by the ER community as a position of sober realism. Not to do so is to live in the fantasy world of denialism.

The notion of an unavoidable 'collapse', in the sense of a cascading deterioration in the carrying capacity of the planet, even if factual, seems pessimistic. In the face of such alarming knowledge, it is understandable that people respond by ignoring or denying the facts or even resigned acceptance. The ER community, in contrast, chooses a different course. Being collapse aware and scientifically aware of the likelihood of collapse, is the beginning of the story for them. Collapse awareness motivates the ER community of change makers to express their values of regenerativity, prosociality, and values-based leadership toward post-collapse opportunities. In their values stance of proactive choice lies the basis for a creative pathway of imagining regenerative possibilities that can restore socio-ecological systems to long-term health. From the ER perspective, developing "collapse awareness" is a way to honestly face the science with creativity, courage, and integrity. In the words of Christiana Figueres, the UN negotiator for the Paris Agreement on Climate Change, this approach combines "outrage and optimism". The ER community's outrage over the lack of action on the scientific facts of global biophysical degradation is the engine that drives their optimism for regenerative possibilities.

Collapse awareness establishes the possibility of choice. For both Joe and JP, this awareness provides a foundation for engaging in regenerative entrepreneurial activity. For the ER community collapse awareness acts as a guiding value for informing conversations, decisions, and formal activities. Rather than dampening motivation to act, recognizing the possibility of systemic economic breakdown motivates and even inspires members to participate in Earth regeneration. The ER community responds to these possibilities with transformative regenerative efforts, to design different pathways for meeting economic and social needs so that the same mistakes of disconnection from nature and aiming to have control over it are not repeated. Both JP and Joe realized that they had the ability to choose which big picture narratives they live by. In simple terms, this is the choice between lives that accept extractive systems based on the instrumentalization of people and nature, or lives that support the emergence of regenerative systems based on the inherent valuing of people and natural systems as ends in themselves. Along with many others in the ER community, Joe and JP have chosen the regenerative path and the concept of collapse awareness plays a key role in motivating that choice of designing pathways to regenerative sustainability.

Prosocial behavior

Both JP and Joe see the practice of prosociality not only a foundational aspect of ER's organizational dynamics but also as an essential element for building networks of regenerative communities. Prosocial process, also called prosocial behavior, has three core assumptions. First, what is in a person's best self-interests is often what is best for their shared interests. There is a lot of overlap between self-interest and community well-being. Second, there are useful design principles that help to align group and individual concerns and collectively balance their interests. Prosociality is the motivation that individuals feel to apply these principles in flourishing together. Third, prosociality and the underlying design principles can be used to network groups across any area or region from the local to the global. In many ways, the value of prosociality, it might also be called extended empathy or compassion, complements the principle of collapse awareness. As previously discussed, collapse awareness recognizes that global society is currently set on a traumatic trajectory of upheaval. Joe and JP see prosociality as a guiding social principle for navigating this journey at the micro and meso levels of the individual, group, and network activities.

In their interviews, both Joe and JP mentioned that in the early build-up phase of ER, they called for healing circles for addressing individual trauma. The purpose here was to give space to each other to learn more about themselves, their past, and to connect more deeply with their values. Furthermore, Joe explains that prosociality requires, "a kind of mindfulness, an awareness of one's motivations, emotions, and assumptions about what social benefits are and why we engage in altruistic behavior". Simply wanting to help others does not ensure good outcomes and being mindful of our own intentions and needs is a crucial aspect of true community service. As Joe puts it, "The practice of mindfulness can be helpful to quieten the ego and bring into focus the values of care and compassion that guide us in our encounters with others and that help us see them in their full being".

Prosocial governance

JP tells a story in which she realized she had a choice to speak up about a crucially important matter. In the preliminary stages of the organization's development, a leadership group was assigned by Joe to give recommendations on ER governance. After serious discussions, the group presented a proposal at a meeting on various options for the governance design of the ER community. The development of the proposal was carried out by a small group of enthusiastic and experienced ER members, but there was no formal process for involving the broad membership of the group. This was something that JP did not agree with; she felt it set a poor example for how ER should exercise its community governance duties and decision-making responsibilities. During the meeting, most people chose to be silent, but JP took the risk to speak up, voice her concerns, and talk about values, responsibilities, and methods for increasing member participation. At the time, this created some internal conflict that impacted on the whole community. She felt that this was a decisive point in the emergence of the ER community, and that it would be a tragedy if this perceived conflict in receiving feedback halted the growth of ER, especially since a core principle and value within ER is collective leadership. She did some further research into the work of Paul Atkins, David Wilson, and Steven Hayes on prosociality, and took up training to be a Prosocial World facilitator. It seemed to her that this approach to "enhancing group functioning" (Atkins et al., 2019, p. VIII) could be a useful tool for connecting the meso level of the group, the micro level of the individual, and the macro level of the community itself.

Subsequently, she organized a 'reflection harvest' session with prosociality as the guiding process. The group all shared ('harvested') their thoughts on what had happened. This resulted in a fruitful session creating a positive ripple effect within ER and many joined with Joe and JP in studying and becoming facilitators for prosocial behavior. Since then, prosociality has been adopted as a core principle within the ER community. JP explained that one clear lesson from this experience was that when individual trauma unconsciously enters the collective domain, it can block community building. Prosociality creates the interpersonal conditions for healing, or, at least, acknowledging the impact of personal trauma. After the reflection harvest, healing circle workshops followed for ER members to share their personal stories and histories. Prosociality at the collective level is built on interpersonal connectedness and trust. JP says that, "In our current social fabric, it's almost impossible to know what's true for others. We must actively ask, listen, and receive them. These are skills that must be cultivated."

Prosocial processes of building empathy, practicing altruistic behavior and reciprocity, and designing for prosociality are systematically included within ER decision-making process and governance structures. Prosociality has given the group important insights, such as the vast importance of reflecting together and deciding what behavior supports the well-being of the community. JP regards the uptake of prosociality and its associated practices as one of the most important developments in building the ER community. The approach has become an indispensable part of ER's governance culture and organizational dynamics and its outreach work of building international networks of regenerative communities.

Extended custodianship

A popular misconception about sustainability is that it is about 'saving the planet': That sustainability is about stopping humanity from endangering the very existence of the planet in pursuit of its unsustainable activities. In many ways, this misconstrued framing of sustainability is another form of anthropocentrism, of placing humanity at the center of the natural world. It is true that humanity is currently the dominant force of planetary change, but humanity does not determine the fate of the whole planet. The planet will continue despite the impact of human activities. What the Anthropocene does put at existential risk is the well-being of human communities and the resilience of the ecological systems on which they depend. ER takes the view that humanity is part of nature and connected to all other beings and species. Human communities should act as stewards, servants, and custodians rather than as owners, managers, and masters. This core value of custodianship is central to ER organizational identity. Instead of viewing nature as a resource to exploit, they view her as their precious relative to care for.

A custodian is a person with responsibility for protecting or taking care of something or keeping something in good condition. The phrase is commonly used to describe the work of physically maintaining a building or area. This is the work of the janitor, a *care-taker*, someone who cares for the integrity of a physical facility. Caretakers keep things tidy, carry out maintenance, and keep services in good order. Their duties include cleaning, repairing, restoring, and replacing damaged natural or built objects. The caretaker values the condition or state of their environment and wants others to do the same. Perhaps the caretaker puts up signs saying "Wet Paint" or "Out of Order" and erects a temporary fence around a garden bed of seedlings or a newly sown lawn to protect the young plants. Another caretaker might provide for a community garden patch or put up some bird nesting boxes. The ER community members similarly feel themselves to be caretakers and custodians, the difference being that the environment they care for is the Earth's biosphere. Their sense of care and responsibility is an extended one that goes beyond the local and the private to include the public commons of the air, the oceans, the water, the forests, that provide ecosystem services to human communities. This is illustrated in many of the episodes of the "ER Podcast", which provides a platform for local ER groups to talk about their bioregional projects. For example, one episode looked at a social-ecological restoration project in the Salish Sea area of the Pacific North-West of the USA. The project involves gathering local communities onto bioregions that need restoration and regeneration. The process is called *restoration camping* and involves doing the actual work of land and ecosystem restoration but also reflection, contemplative evaluation, and relationship building. Participants camp in a designated area, called a biocultural field station, and do the manual work of restoration but also think about and discuss with each other their role as stewards and caretakers for bioregional systems.

It is not only the extended spatial responsibilities that are involved here, but also extended circles of temporal responsibilities. Members see themselves as having obligations to future generations as much as to present ones. Voicing values that come out of this spatially and temporally extended sense of care can be a risky business. These altruistic values run counter to much of what modern economics assume to be natural. But the innovation of how values are expressed is also part of the enjoyment and attraction that the ER members feel in doing this kind of work. This extended view of identifying oneself as a custodian of Planet Earth is a helpful perspective from which to challenge and question established patterns in community and economic life that are contributing to harmful levels of ecological deterioration. An extended sense of responsibility for the Earth and its future generations might also help us imagine new forms of regenerative living and new kinds of community-based and social entrepreneurship.

Developmental entrenchment and regenerative design

Civic education is one of the core functions of the ER organization. It sees this area of work as enabling the global development of regenerative possibilities for networks of bioregional projects. Bioregional networks are systems of regionally and digitally connected landscape-based communities who work and live to regenerate systems of human and biophysical location. Bioregions are the units of global regeneration. ER provides the educational tools for this to take place. Examples of this kind of educational work include exploring the latest Earth system science findings, developing critical perspectives on the causes of global environmental and social crises, and designing regenerative collaborations. One core analytical concept that ER uses in its educational courses is called *developmental entrenchment*. Developmental entrenchment is the idea that societies will sometimes maladaptively use established approaches to address new problems even when they do not work. This is similar to the epigram, often attributed to Einstein: "You can't solve a problem using the same logic that caused it." For example, economic theories and methods arising from previous periods in history can hinder the ability to respond creatively to new economic problems. If fundamentally new environmental circumstances emerge that challenge social institutions and practices, it is likely that old strategies will not produce the requisite solutions. This is particularly true when those challenges emerge rapidly, are complex, and put at risk the vested interests of established centers of power and wealth. Responses to climate change are examples of this kind of developmental entrenchment. Such challenges can result in ideological fixations and cultural practices that are maladaptive. Developmental entrenchment does not always result in maladaptive responses; when it does, however, it is very resistant to modification.

ER sees the influence of developmental entrenchment at play in the assumption that exponential economic growth is needed to underwrite sustainability-oriented innovations and investments. An unquestioned belief in economic growth as the key to achieving progress and higher living standards might have been developmentally appropriate when the Earth had a seemingly boundless supply of natural resources to do business with. However, this point is long gone and the pursuit of unending exponential economic growth is known to be a driving factor behind global ecological destruction (Jackson, 2017; Stiglitz, Sen, & Fitoussi, 2009). Nonetheless, growth remains a fixation for global business and there are many institutional and legal structures in place that require public companies to pursue short-term growth strategies. The critical perspective of ER courses sees current economic systems as locked into a maladaptive set of extractive business practices that are unsuitable for contemporary circumstances and unhealthy for human communities and the biophysical systems they depend on. Growth-centric developmental entrenchment encourages an ideology of placing financial outcomes before people and planet-related outcomes. It encourages short-termism and discourages long-term entrepreneurial thinking (Edwards, 2021). Many of ER's courses and online discussions are aimed at designing regenerative pathways that do not depend on these entrenched logics.

Concepts such as developmental entrenchment constitute an important part of ER culture. These analytical tools inform its critical analysis and ethical critique of mainstream economic, business, and legal systems. ER sees these kinds of intellectual tools as fundamental to the development of regenerative culture and regenerative forms of economic activity. To think in intergenerational time scales is a key factor in all forms of sustainability, especially regenerative forms. In questioning the status quo of entrenched practices, regenerative entrepreneurs are working to upgrade the software that keeps human culture adaptive to the needs of the present.

Design school for regenerating earth

After leaving ER in 2022, Joe Brewer and other participants from the ER community started a membership-based organization called the Design School for Regenerating Earth. This educational organization shares all the core values and goals of ER, but focuses directly on the task of regenerative landscape design. Taking inspiration from Brewer's book *The Design Pathway for Regenerating Earth*, the school works through its members on the ground in bioregions to build community in that region and to link it with other regenerative projects. It is this grounded regional work, combining design teaching with bioregional networking, that is the core work of the design school. Joe sees the work of the Design School for Regenerating Earth as another avenue for supporting those who fully accept the global environmental, social, and economic challenges that characterize contemporary times.

Core insights

In the following we describe some core insights that we distilled from this case of ER and its founding entrepreneurs, Joe and JP. We focus on the insights gained through applying the GVV lenses of *Choice* and *Values*. We also include other findings that emerged from our analysis of the interviews and case materials and connect these with core aspects of the GVV approach to ethics.

Performative ethics – Voicing our values to become who we want to be

Practical personal ethics is about engaging in conversations that help us create preferred futures. This is a performative approach to ethics, that is, in voicing our concerns and dreams with others, we actively set up the social conditions that help us enact those dreams. Through communication we create, design, and shape the futures that we eventually inhabit and which, in turn, shape us. This kind of ethics lies outside of descriptive explanations of what *is* the case and goes well beyond normative rules and calculations about what *ought* to be the case. Instead, regenerative entrepreneurs are making experiments with the performative world of what *might* be the case. Joe, JP, and others within the ER and Design School for Regenerating Earth communities are involved in a similar kind of ethical journey. They are experimenting with a new kind of moral vision that sees humanity's current economic activities as morally indefensible. The conversational, educational, and developmental activities of these organizations are performative experiments with new identities and practices. Joe and JP, with the other ER and design school members, co-create their realizing future possibilities by enacting what they refer to as "design pathways for regenerating Earth". They have chosen to be critical and science-based in their thinking, prosocial in their relations, imaginative in their designing, and regenerative in their vision. These qualities have enabled them to connect deeply with their values of regenerativity, with the persons they desire to be, and the futures they choose to work toward.

Regenerative visions and science

Regenerative organizations take the findings of Earth system science seriously. Their organizational values are shaped by the facts that this science is establishing about the cause of global environmental crises and their implications for human societies. ER and the Design School for Regenerating Earth advocate for a radical form of regenerativity that plants the seeds of transformation in local communities. They radically question many of the basic assumptions of modern economic systems on scientific grounds. From the ER perspective, its values are based on facts rather than in opposition to them. ER values are informed by the facts of climate change, biodiversity loss, plastic pollution, the science of bio-physical tipping points, and changing land use patterns. The values of regenerative organizations are neither intuitive inspirations divorced from contemporary realities nor are they purely emotional reactions to faddish concerns. These regenerative communities and its entrepreneurial leaders ask ethical questions about our responsibilities that are informed by the science. Together with conceptual tools like the notion of development entrenchment, they critically investigate current practices and offer different cultural stories, different choices to those they have inherited. The regenerative vision that these engaged change makers present is radically different from commercialized market-based capitalism. However, the ER community would argue that their vision, in contrast to the conventional world of extractive commercialism, is firmly based on the science and informed by ethical values where humanity thrives within the means of a regenerative and living planet.

The paradox of choice

Throughout this chapter we have explored the GVV pillar of choice. It takes imagination and determination to finding the possibility of choice within an economic system that is generally assumed to be unchangeable. The designed educational activities of the ER community are a kind of habitual practising of choice in that they demand a repeated cycle of questioning current pathways and creating possibilities. Out of these activities the many ER groups build up what might be seen as an 'ethical momentum' for establishing regenerative futures. The new paths that are opened for practice become possible, what is deliberately and repeatedly chosen becomes the routine, until eventually it becomes the default pathway. The ER leaders and facilitators closely identify with the purpose and ethical values that their organization works to enact. Identity and choice can be very tightly aligned when this level of commitment is present. During our interviews with JP, she once joked that, "Being part of this community does not feel like a choice anymore". This is the paradox of choice – the dynamic between deliberate choice and committed identification. Choice is essential for creating possibility and innovation and committed involvement is essential for building those possibilities into something substantive.

Building community and finding allies

Entrepreneurs and entrepreneurial communities need allies to be sustainable. Finding allies who share similar goals and motivations is a vital element in building organizations that express our deepest values. Both Joe and JP desperately wanted to be members of a community that shared their worldviews and values and which supported them to engage meaningfully in regenerative work. So, they worked to build those communities and create social environments that supported them. The act of surrounding themselves with people who share similar purposes and values has been a critical ingredient in these entrepreneurs' lives. For Joe and JP, the entrepreneurial work of establishing an alternative community, to find a social setting where they can pursue careers, has been inseparable from their own personal need to live out their core values.

Prosociality

Prosociality encourages people to discover their values, to give space and time to themselves and other so that collaborations can flourish. The process of prosociality and holding space for personal discoveries are intended to develop healthy communities and rewarding personal lives and there are many points of connection between prosocial process for achieving that and the GVV pillars, especially those of *Values* and *Choice*. Atkins, Wilson, and Hayes (2019) have described the core principles of prosocial behavior. They state that:

> The Prosocial process strives to build upon the passion and motivation that arises from acting in line with one's own needs, values, and aims, while also satisfying the needs, values, and aims of others in the group, and the collective as a whole.
>
> (Atkins et al., 2019, pp. 3–4)

Applying prosociality to create a "culture that supports everybody having a voice" (Atkins et al., 2019, p. 136) has clear parallels with GVV approach to ethical leadership and "listening for values in others" (Gentile, 2016, p. 109).

Challenges and opportunities

Business ethics is typically thought of as the study of how to stop people and their businesses and organizations from doing harmful things. It is rarely, if ever, framed as the study of how people can grasp opportunities to do something good. GVV is not only about resolving ethical dilemmas, but also about taking hold of opportunities to generate benefits for others. Regenerative entrepreneurs focus on this second understanding of ethical action. To paraphrase Kate Raworth, regenerative entrepreneurs aim to maximize the generation of benefits rather than minimize the extractive harms. This does not mean they ignore the harms. In fact, the ER community begins its journey with a thorough education in the scientific facts about the dire state of the planet's biophysical health. But once that foundation is established, they then create possibilities for positive action. Their work is not to avoid unsustainable activity but rather to embark on possibilities for Earth regeneration. And personal regeneration is part of this process as well. The learning involved in prosociality, becoming Earth custodians, developing an extended sense of responsibility to nature and other species are all opportunities for personal as well as community growth. Even as it fully recognizes the complexity of creating a better life for all and reducing the burden on the life-support systems of the planet, the ER and the Design School for Regenerating Earth communities and their entrepreneurial leaders are intent on designing regenerative pathways that balance and integrate these ethical commitments.

Case questions

1. How did the characteristics of collapse awareness help ER develop a sense of choice in their organizational culture?
2. How did Joe's and JP's values provide guidance and inspiration for their entrepreneurial activities?
3. Given your understanding of the ER organization and their view that collapse is a real possibility but also as an incentive to act, what are your own views on 'collapse'?
4. How have you understood the relationship between ethical crises and grasping ethical opportunities?
5. How has the process of identification with Earth Regenerator values enabled members to explore regenerativity?
6. Explain the paradox of choice in your own words and discuss how it contributes to regenerative entrepreneurship.

Workshop exercises

Exercise 1:   Personal Backcasting – What choice do we have?

May your choices reflect your hopes, not your fears.

– Nelson Mandela

The challenge

What choices do you need to make to move toward regenerative goals in your personal life?[3] For example, how can you contribute to restoring human and natural systems in our own neighborhoods over the long term? This is a challenging task to say the least. People are social beings, influenced by the norms and cultures (and developmental entrenchments) that characterize the social situations of the workplace. In this exercise we practice using the method of backcasting at the individual level to find ways of putting our values and ideals into practical actions.

Time: 2 hours

Quote: "The two most important days in life are the day you born and the day you find out why you were born." – Mark Twain

Purpose of the exercise: To use backcasting to clarify what choices you need to move toward regenerative goals or activities in your life and work.

Structure of Exercise:
1. **Opening invitation:**
    Invite students to ask themselves these questions. What do you value and how might you express these values in regenerative goals that you would like to explore in your life and work?
2. **Materials and spaces:**
    Can be online or onsite. Seating arrangements are flexible.
3. **Group participation and configuration:**
    Uses the "think, write, pair, share" technique that moves from individual reflection to pairwise discussion to group discussion.

4. **Sequence of Steps and Time Allocation**:
   a. Write a brief paragraph of 2–3 sentences that describes a regenerative goal that you want to achieve in your working life. After that, work backwards to figure out the necessary choices you need to make at each step to stay on track to achieve that goal. (15 minutes) (For more on backcasting see Robèrt et al., 2012.)
   b. Share this paragraph with another class partner by: i) reading it out ii) asking for their thoughts on your regenerative goal and the backcasting choices you have stepped out, iii) then amend your paragraph in response to your partner's comments. (2 × 15 minutes = 30 minutes).
   c. Some prompting questions: Are your choice clearly setting up a feasible pathway to your regenerative goal? Are there better alternative choices that could help you to follow and achieve your purpose?
   d. Share your thoughts about your purpose and the choices you need to make to achieve it with a small group of four. (4 × 5 minutes each = 20 minutes)
   e. Convene as a class for class discussion. (15 min)

   Total time with 10-minute break = 90 minutes

5. **Tips and Traps**:
   - Provide a backcasting diagram to each student.
   - Break the backcasting period into 2–5-year timeslots.

6. **Variations:**
   If running online use breakout groups for the paired and groups discussion steps.

   If running for executive education class, break the task down into career opportunities.

7. **Suggested extension materials:**
   https://www.youtube.com/watch?v=J10CAkkAHFQ
   https://www.youtube.com/watch?v=DeDm-HTFuiY
   https://evviva.ai/use-back-casting-to-build-an-abundant-life/

Exercise 2:   Valuing my Values

Open your arms to change but don't let go of your values.
– Dalai Lama

The challenge

To make a clear and vivid declaration from your heart about the values you intend to live by. The values may pertain to any area of your life – personal life, your work, the organization you work in, or your community. The task here is to reflect on your values and see what place they have in your life. Creating such a clear vision of your values can help to make them real, to enact them in everyday life.

What does this exercise make possible?

When you are clear about your values, you can focus your energy and act on what is most important to you. Your actions consistently answer the question "What would someone with my values do next, standing right where I am standing?" The clearer our values, the more opportunities we will find to act on and express our values in pragmatic and skilful ways.

Time:

2 × 15 minutes a day for 7 days, once at the beginning and once at the end of the course.

Structure of Exercise:

Keep a paper diary for seven days in which you describe your values and what impact they have on the choices you make during the day.

1. **Opening invitation:**
    This exercise is to help you get a better sense of what is meaningful and important to you. This will help in making the big decisions and in shaping the social environments that shape you.

2. **Materials and spaces:**
    You can do this exercise anywhere, but you will gain most value if you make some entries in a natural environment, for example, outside during a walk or sitting in a park. Use a pen and paper to do the exercise to minimize other distractions from devices such as your computer, tablet, or phone.

3. **Group participation and configuration:**
    If you are willing, share it with someone who can support you to make your vision a reality.

4. **Sequence of Steps and Time Allocation:**
    a.   At the beginning of the course, over a period of seven days, make a diary entry of around 50–100 words every day that states/describes one of your core values and the importance it has in your life.

b. After the last entry on the seventh day, read over what you have written and reflect on what how these values will shape the decisions you make about your future. Makes some brief notes about these reflections.

c. Type out all your diary entries into a computer document and submit to the class teacher for Pass/Fail assessment (Criteria for passing is that you complete the exercise).

d. Repeat the exercise at the end of the course.

e. Discuss what the exercise meant for you in a final class discussion.

5. **Tips and Traps:**
   - The trap is that some students will not find the exercise useful while others will be fully engaged. Discuss this in class before running the exercise.
   - Try to find ways to make the exercise relevant to students lives. For example, get some businesspeople and entrepreneurs into class who will commit to doing the exercise with the students.

6. **Variations:**
   - Run the exercise just once and discuss in class the following week.
   - The exercise can be done online or onsite.
   - Make it part of the assessment activities for the course.

7. **Suggested extension materials:**
   - Set some reading and watching of GVV articles and videos specifically concerned with values.
   - https://ethicsunwrapped.utexas.edu/video/pillar-1-values
   - https://ethicsunwrapped.utexas.edu/video/moral-muteness

8. **Other Resources:**
   Earth Regenerators: https://earth-regenerators.mn.co/about
   Pro-Social Behavior: https://www.sciencedirect.com/topics/social-sciences/prosocial-behavior

---

Notes

1 In 2022, the founder of the community organization *Earth Regenerators* (ER) left to establish a new member-based organization called the *Design School for Regenerating Earth*. Both organizations have the joint purpose of

supporting regenerative design education and hands-on bioregional projects. We will concentrate on ER in this case but both organizations share the regenerative characteristics discussed here and both are the result of the values-based activities and conversations of Joe Brewer and other leaders from these regenerative organizations.

2 A stakeholder is a person or group of people who have something that they and others value at stake in the operations of an organization. A rightholder is a person or group of people whose basic human rights are being impacted on be the organization's operations.

3 Here are some examples of regenerative behaviors: compost all home vegetable & plant waste; financial support for regenerative businesses; find employment in a regenerative business; support social and political policies that target regenerativity; find regenerative agriculture products that you can access; minimise purchases of fast fashion and other short products; use public transport instead of car travel; walk or bicycle wherever possible; start regenerative gardening; invest in regenerative start-ups; move your pension into long-term sustainability investments; stop travelling by air and use trains; research regenerative products in your local area, stop buying more stuff (sufficiency in purchasing); don't just recycle – refuse, rethink, reuse, and restore.

References

Armstrong McKay, D. I., Staal, A., Abrams, J. F., Winkelmann, R., Sakschewski, B., Loriani, S., ... Lenton, T. M. (2022). Exceeding 1.5°C global warming could trigger multiple climate tipping points. *Science, 377*(6611), 7950. doi:10.1126/science.abn7950

Atkins, P. W., Wilson, D. S., & Hayes, S. C. (2019). *Prosocial: Using Evolutionary Science to Build Productive, Equitable, and Collaborative Groups.* Oakland, California: New Harbinger Publications.

Bar-On, Y. M., Phillips, R., & Milo, R. (2018). The biomass distribution on Earth. *Proceedings of the National Academy of Sciences, 115*(25), 6506. doi:10.1073/pnas.1711842115

Bradshaw, C. J., Ehrlich, P. R., Beattie, A., Ceballos, G., Crist, E., Diamond, J., ... Harte, M. E. (2021). Underestimating the challenges of avoiding a ghastly future. *Frontiers in Conservation Science, 1,* 9.

Brewer, J. (2021). *The Design Pathway for Regenerating Earth.* Barichara, Columbia: Earth Regenerators Press.

Brovkin, V., Brook, E., Williams, J. W., Bathiany, S., Lenton, T. M., Barton, M., ... Yu, Z. (2021). Past abrupt changes, tipping points and cascading impacts in the Earth system. *Nature Geoscience, 14*(8), 550–558. doi:10.1038/s41561-021-00790-5

Butzer, K. W. (2012). Collapse, environment, and society. *Proceedings of the National Academy of Sciences, 109*(10), 3632–3639. doi:10.1073/pnas.1114845109

Ceballos, G., Ehrlich, P. R., & Dirzo, R. (2017). Biological annihilation via the ongoing sixth mass extinction signaled by vertebrate population losses and declines. *Proceedings of the National Academy of Sciences, 114*(30), E6089–E6096. doi:10.1073/pnas.1704949114

Cowie, R. H., Bouchet, P., & Fontaine, B. (2022). The sixth mass extinction: Fact, fiction or speculation? *Biological Reviews, 97*(2), 640–663. doi:10.1111/brv.12816

Edwards, M. G. (2021). The growth paradox, sustainable development, and business strategy. *Business Strategy and the Environment, 30*(7), 3079–3094. doi:10.1002/bse.2790

Fisher, M. (2009). *Capitalist Realism: Is There No Alternative?* London: John Hunt Publishing.

Gentile, M. C. (2016). Listening for values. *Humanist Management Journal, 1,* 107–111.

IPCC, Pörtner, H.-O., Roberts, D. C., Poloczanska, E. S., Mintenbeck, K., Tignor, M., ... Okem, A. (Eds.). (2022). *Climate Change 2022: Impacts, Adaptation and Vulnerability. Contribution of Working Group II to the Sixth Assessment Report of the Intergovernmental Panel on Climate Change.* Cambridge, UK: Cambridge University Press.

Jackson, T. (2017). *Prosperity without Growth: Foundations for the Economy of Tomorrow* (2nd ed.). London: Routledge.

Lenton, T. M., Rockström, J., Gaffney, O., Rahmstorf, S., Richardson, K., Steffen, W., & Schellnhuber, H. J. (2019). Climate tipping points - Too risky to bet against. *Nature, 575,* 592–595.

Persson, L., Carney Almroth, B. M., Collins, C. D., Cornell, S., de Wit, C. A., Diamond, M. L., ... Hauschild, M. Z. (2022). Outside the safe operating space of the planetary boundary for novel entities. *Environmental Science & Technology, 56*(3), 1510–1521. doi:10.1021/acs.est.1c04158

Robèrt, K.-H., Göran, B., Ny, H., Byggeth, S., Missimer, M., Connel, T., ... Oldmark, J. (2012). *Sustainability Handbook: Planning Strategically towards Sustainability.* Stockholm: Studentlitteratur.

Steffen, W., Richardson, K., Rockström, J., Cornell, S. E., Fetzer, I., Bennett, E. M., ... de Wit, C. A. (2015). Planetary boundaries: Guiding human development on a changing planet. *Science, 347*(6223), 1–10.

Stiglitz, J. E., Sen, A., & Fitoussi, J. (2009). *Report by the Commission on the Measurement of Economic Performance and Social Progress.* Retrieved from http://www.stiglitz-sen-fitoussi.fr/

Wang-Erlandsson, L., Tobian, A., van der Ent, R. J., Fetzer, I., te Wierik, S., Porkka, M., ... Rockström, J. (2022). A planetary boundary for green water. *Nature Reviews Earth & Environment, 3*(6), 380–392. doi:10.1038/s43017-022-00287-8

Willcock, S., Cooper, G. S., Addy, J., & Dearing, J. A. (2023). Earlier collapse of Anthropocene ecosystems driven by multiple faster and noisier drivers. *Nature Sustainability.* doi:10.1038/s41893-023-01157-x

4

COMMONLAND AND NORMALIZING THE NEW

This chapter investigates how two regenerative entrepreneurs working for the organization Commonland create a shared narrative of regenerativity among multiple stakeholder groups using their "4 Returns Framework for Landscape Restoration". Commonland's mission is to regenerate degraded landscapes into thriving ecosystems, resilient communities, and responsible economies. The story of how Commonland was birthed by visionary tropical ecologist and entrepreneur Willem Ferwerda is presented and analyzed using the GVV pillar of *Normalization*. Practical insights are extracted from Commonland's ongoing work to embed, and therefore normalize, a holistic approach to landscape restoration and community building. It is hoped that this will provide inspiration, references, and guidance for students and others interested in regenerative entrepreneurship. In the following pages we describe the founding of Commonland, provide a GVV perspective on how Willem worked with opportunities and overcome barriers and obstacles to make Commonland a success. The insights from the case also offer some new perspectives on how GVV can be used to work strategically to scale up and scale deep social innovations like regenerative landscape renewal.

DOI: 10.4324/9781003330660-4

THE CASE OF *COMMONLAND* IN BRIEF

Organization name: Commonland
Year of founding: 2013
Website: www.Commonland.com
Type of organization: A not-for-profit foundation for restoring degraded landscapes and regenerate communities using a holistic approach to landscape restoration called the '4 Returns Framework', of economic, social, environmental, and inspirational returns.
Purpose/mission of organization: To make holistic landscape restoration the new norm by restoring 100 million hectares of the world's degraded landscapes by 2040. To move from an economic model that maximizes profit to one that protects, restores, and strengthens the environment for future generations.
Industry/community sector: Landscape and community regeneration
Services: Knowledge management, network development, data management, facilitation of collaboration, program design, leveraging finance, project management, monitoring and evaluation.
Locations: Based in Amsterdam, The Netherlands with operations and projects in 20 countries across all six continents.
Impact and achievements: In 2022 Commonland's impact as measured by their 4 Returns Framework was as follows: Inspiration – 2,650 partners connected globally, 5.7 million people were communicated with through (online) media, documentaries, participation in local pilots and research projects, or participation in workshops, webinars and festivals. Social – 850 direct and indirect jobs created. Environment – 44,000 hectares of degraded land under direct regeneration (improved soil, water, biodiversity, vegetative biomass). Economic – 36 regenerative businesses set up.

The Commonland foundation

Commonland is an international not-for-profit foundation that was established in 2013 to implement large-scale landscape restoration projects across the world. A foundation is an organization that is legally constituted to achieve a particular purpose but does not have a defined owner. Commonland was founded to build sustainable communities and landscapes through implementing a new balance between ecology, economics, and community development in order to build more equitable and environmentally sustainable societies. The organization was founded by Willem Ferwerda and supported by scientific institutions and several entrepreneurs who shared a vision of how to do things differently. The founding actors structured Commonland so that it was not profit margins that drove the strategies of the organization or even the career motivations of its members, but rather the real needs of natural systems and the communities that depended on them that inspired optimism and energy for the initiative.

Regenerative entrepreneurs face ethical dilemmas because sustainability requires significant changes to the Business-As-Usual (BAU) approach to conducting commerce. Consequently, Commonland leaders and staff have faced many demanding situations where voicing values was essential for maintaining the integrity of their mission. In this chapter, we explore some of these situations using the GVV lens of normalizing ethical challenges. This lens is crucially important in the challenge of transitioning to sustainable futures. To avoid the worst impacts of the environmental challenges that societies now face, the aspirations of regenerative organizations such as Commonland may well need to become the norm, the default mode of business purposes. Shifting whole economies through normalizing the regenerative mission and vision that Commonland utilizes to achieve its purpose is an extremely ambitious goal. However, transitioning from the current extractive modes of economic activity to more prudent ones must be accomplished over the next few decades if the turmoil of cascading disruptions across planetary biophysical systems is to be avoided (Brovkin et al., 2021; Buldyrev, Parshani, Paul, Stanley, & Havlin, 2010; Lenton et al., 2019).

In this chapter, we will dig into and find examples to illustrate Commonland's business philosophy and strategy and see how, from the very beginning, its founders and guiding entrepreneurs worked to normalize a social-ecological view of development among industry stakeholders. We aim to gain some insights into how Commonland and its leaders have effectively voiced their values to shift how we understand economic prosperity and how it can support the development and flourishing of human communities and the natural systems on which they depend. To do this we consider the significant moments in Commonland's emergence and analyze the experiences of two entrepreneurs intimately involved in success over the decade since its founding. So, let us start at the beginning when founder Willem Ferwerda was a young child growing up in the Netherlands.

Willem Ferwerda: "We are all part of nature"

Willem was born in the Netherlands in 1959. The young Willem had an extraordinarily strong connection to nature throughout his upbringing. He was raised to enjoy being outdoors, to be curious about living things and to experience the beauty and power of the natural world. When Willem was eight years old, he had a simple yet profound insight into his own inextricable connection to nature. He and his father were hiking around a lake when suddenly they saw adults screaming and throwing rocks at a snake. Willem did not share people's fear of the snake; instead, he was curious to see it up close. He loved animals and, although he had previously only seen a snake in a zoo, he approached the creature, which turned out to be a harmless grass snake. He looked it in the eyes with an open heart and an unspoken, "What are they doing to you?" Willem felt the mirrored response from the snake's perspective. These people are throwing rocks at themselves, he thought to himself. They are unnecessarily harming another living creature, harming something that they themselves are part of. At eight years of age Willem experienced this deep sense of connection to nature, which some might even see in spiritual or transcendent terms. An insight that shifts the individual perspective beyond the ego and into a feeling that one's being is inseparable from the natural world in which it is embedded. Powerful experiences like this can shape how we interact with nature throughout our lives, and they give us opportunities to think and plan for how we act when encountering similar situations.

Unfortunately, this intimate experience of nature is something that is experienced by fewer and fewer people today because of our increasingly urbanized lifestyles. More than half of the world's population now live in cities, meaning that they are cut off from everyday experiences of the natural world. In some ways the origins of Commonland are to be found in Willem's portentous experience and instinct for "reconnecting to the biosphere" (Folke et al., 2011). It is also important to note, however, that this is no romantic quest or infantile wish for simpler times. We will see in Willem's and Commonland's story that reconnection with nature plays a fundamentally integrative role in the foundation's work in that it consolidates and embodies economic, social, and psychological aspirations.

This insight of deep interconnectedness with nature became a guiding light for Willem's entire adult life. He studied biology and specialized in tropical ecology and environmental science, first at the Free University and later at the University of Amsterdam and the Universidad Nacional in Bogotá, Colombia. He specialized in tropical ecology, and the interaction of poor farmers in clearing virgin tropical mountain ecosystems (páramos) and the recuperation of these ecosystems after people left. He worked with the International Union for Conservation of Nature (IUCN) for 17 years on a multitude of projects around the world, where he learned about the impact through funding 1,500 conservation projects in the tropics and set up a business network on nature (Leaders for Nature) with parties McKinsey and Egon Zehnder. He gained knowledge through the experience of being grounded in social communities and ecological localities. He learned first-hand the importance of integrating different stakeholder perspectives for facilitating nature conservation. For 12 years, from 2000 to 2012, Willem was Executive Director of The International Union for Conservation of Nature (IUCN) Netherlands and he was successful in helping the Dutch chapter of that environmental NGO become one of the most important international conservation organizations in The Netherlands. He loved his work but strongly felt the need for an even deeper understanding of ecology to be spread among diverse groups of stakeholders, including farmers, businesspeople, and town dwellers. Knowledge about how nature works and understanding our relationship to nature is essential for making the right decisions. He wanted to create both a practical means and a narrative framework for bringing diverse stakeholders together to restore both natural landscapes *and* areas impacted by human activities, such as agricultural lands, local towns, and regional zones. He wanted every stakeholder to be guided by the realization that we are *part* of nature rather than *apart* from it and allow that realization to guide our economic and social planning and decision-making.

Willem left his work at IUCN Netherlands in 2012, when he took a sabbatical year to speak with farmers, investors, politicians, ecologists, and other stakeholders to understand what motivated them, what stimulated their thinking, and what drove their actions on environmental issues. Willem already knew that economic systems should be about creating and sustaining the real value of our global and local life support systems, but the question was: *how should we do that?* Ecological conservation and restoration needed to be integrated into the work and thinking of all stakeholders if transformational change were to occur. How we think and work with nature starts with our internal psychology, and this was something that needed to be emphasized in the framework. Willem came to see that, beyond the three often-cited capitals – financial, social, and ecological capital – a fourth source of capital was desperately needed, and he knew what that missing piece was – inspiration. It is inspiration, hope, and optimism that drive people's planning, investment, and expectations for the future. Why grow food if there is no hope for a harvest? Why invest money, time, or energy if you don't believe value will be increased and returned to all those who take the risk. Why commit to anything if it is not inspiring? With these insights in hand Willem set out on the journey of establishing an organization that could truly embody his values.

Simon Moolenaar: "Signs of hope"

Simon Moolenaar is Director of Knowledge, Education, and Innovation at Commonland. He joined the organization in 2015 and was initially brought in to establish Commonland's community engagement and educational activities. Simon holds a master's degree in environmental sciences and has a PhD in the sustainable management of agricultural ecosystems. He has a professional background in integrated landscape management where he has worked as a consultant in landscape regeneration projects. He had worked to align partners' interests through mediation to identify and agree on scientific insights and common benefits for practitioners, business professionals and policy makers. This was a perfect background for Commonland, where aligning the interests of stakeholders in the context of a landscape approach was central to their project goals. Hence, it was no coincidence that Simon was attracted to work with Commonland.

As an environmental scientist, Simon was aware of the basic causes of unfolding global sustainability crises, and he was particularly motivated by a keen sense of urgency to work in landscape and community restoration. Simon found special interest in the food–water–energy nexus and how improving the sustainability of the food production and agricultural sectors could address environmental crises occurring at larger scales. Working with these topics, Simon felt he could help create "signs of hope" at the meso-level of long-term organizational initiatives to help landscapes (constituted of both communities and ecosystems) transition to a more sustainable operational basis. Working with the keystone topics of land and water management, ecosystem services, land use and food networks, Simon felt he could make a real impact on issues of drought, degradation, and desertification and make a positive difference through regenerative and restorative strategies based on resilient business model development, including the return of hope and inspiration. By doing active research in landscapes, establishing digital learning platforms, and creating experience-based learning opportunities, Simon works with Commonland to communicate and catalyze its business model among different stakeholder groups, including business students, development organizations, regional communities, and sustainability professionals.

The creation of Commonland

In 2013 Willem connected several players in his organizational network, including the IUCN Commission on Ecosystem Management, the Rotterdam School of Management, and the COmON Foundation led by Wijnand Pon, and brought them together to establish Commonland. Leveraging the knowledge, social network, and shared trust that this supportive network provided, Commonland aimed to develop landscape restoration partnerships based on timeframes of twenty years and more. It began by scaling up some existing restoration projects by developing collaborations that would generate very long-term investment returns. But there were many obstacles to be overcome to secure this long-term funding. Willem had to convince the marketplace of possible partners that the long-term timeframes and the holistic goals he wanted to achieve were feasible. He had to find villagers, farmers, investors, and local businesses who held values and visions that aligned with Commonland's core approach. To invest over such an extended period and to prioritize social-ecological goals before financial ones was different and personal trust was needed to get communities on board.

Extremely patient investors and partners were needed for the long investment timeframe that was a core aspect of Commonland's work. Conventional business venturing often aims for financial returns to be built into a business model's short-term planning with a significant level of return, if not profit, often expected within one or two fiscal quarters. Nature, however, works in much longer timeframes. To create regenerative return in social and ecological capital, the minimum timeframe would need to be much longer, years and even decades longer. Willem needed a simple structure for communicating his ideas about long timeframes, inspiration, and holistic landscape renewal and, after some years of thought and experimentation, he finally distilled all this into the 4 Returns Framework (Ferwerda, 2015) which became Commonland's core investment and motivational vision (Commonland, 2022).

The 4 Returns were the economic, social, environmental, and inspirational rewards that stakeholders could receive from their long-term pecuniary and non-pecuniary investments. The 4 Returns Framework combined these investment returns with 5 Elements of landscape restoration; the latter included things such as developing local partnerships, reaching shared understandings, co-creating plans, collective learning, and ensuring effective implementation. All these process components were targeted toward successful landscape restoration for three zones of a landscape: the natural zone of bio-physical integrity; the combined zone of regenerative agriculture and community resilience; and the economic zone of sustainable economic productivity. Together, the 4 Returns, the 5 Elements, the 3 Zones, and the timeframe of 20 years laid the basic framework for Commonland's business model (referred to as the "4 Returns Framework"). Willem had been developing this framework for some time and had practiced communicating it in many forms before settling on its basic structure. The 4 Returns was a concise way of communicating a process of change, a model of investment returns, and a landscape approach to social-ecological regeneration. The narrative of the 4 Returns set out a bold vision, but the boldness needed to be anchored in economic and social realities. Conveying the 4 Returns narrative in a persuasive and powerful way presented a major communication challenge considering the funding environments Commonland had to compete and operate within.

Willem wanted to find the right people to work with and thus establish a multidisciplinary team. An organization such as Commonland required people who were independent thinkers and doers from diverse backgrounds who could co-create the leadership of the organization, and these people needed to be fully on board with the organization's vision, mission, and guiding values. Irrespective of their professional suitability, experience, and educational qualifications, if he could not connect with his staff on the fundamental levels of why a fully regenerative perspective was needed for a restorative project, then it was simply not going to work. Fortunately, the first appointment Willem recruited was business consultant Michiel de Man, who became the Director of Strategy. Michiel was a key recruit in terms of founding the strategic direction of Commonland. Soon after 2015, soil scientist Simon Moolenaar became part of the senior management team. With the team in place, the work of putting ideas into practice began.

The 4 Returns in practice – Altiplano Estepario

Simon states that Commonland's activities are "targeted towards connecting economy and ecology in a broad sense that utilizes a landscape approach that can address multiple issues in an integrated way". By demonstrating the possibilities of regenerative sustainability across restorative projects that involve issues of land use, community and family collaborations, and economic benefits, Commonland engages with the most important form of investment return – inspiration. Through establishing a pipeline of restorative landscape projects, the organization brings to stakeholders an awareness of the investment possibilities offered by this new way of doing things.

Commonland's pragmatic focus can be illustrated by one of their main projects in Spain. In 2014, Commonland mobilized farmers, entrepreneurs, and other stakeholders in Altiplano Estepario in Southern Spain. This region, which spans a million hectares, has been heavily impacted by generations of poor agricultural practices, land degradation, deforestation, drought, and climate change. The region receives less than 80 mm (about 3.15 in) of annual rainfall and there is little vegetation to stop runoff from eroding topsoils and washing them into the local streams, and eventually into the Mediterranean. Together with their partners, Commonland embarked on an ambitious initiative to halt desertification and restore sustainably productive drylands using the 4 Returns Framework. The landscape model of land restoration that the 4 Returns is based on works within the defining bioregional limits of the geographical integrity and ecosystem features of a region, for example, a river system, a plateau, or a mountain range. A recent report from the UN Decade on Ecosystem Restoration states that:

> The "landscape approach" seeks to balance competing stakeholder demands in a mosaic of different management approaches, to supply a full range of natural, social and economic returns.
>
> (Dudley et al., 2021, p. 4)

The Altiplano plateau was a perfect bioregion for Commonland to work in. Simon explains the choice of this area as follows.

> The first and main reason to start a project in this region of Spain was the quality of the people on the ground who could drive the process. They were already active in various entrepreneurial projects, some restoration related. Second, the rain fed almonds grown in this region presented a strong potential business case. And third, a restoration project in this region offered good possibilities for scalability.
>
> (Moolenaar et al., 2023)

They started by creating a vision of the landscape with a group of local farmers, conservationist entrepreneurs in November 2014 for 2034, 20+ years from the project's initiation. This period of a minimum of twenty years is a standard "project" planning period for Commonland collaborations. A minimum of twenty years provides enough time for ecological and economic restoration. This extended period also signals to stakeholders, who are often farmers, farming families, and local regional businesses, that Commonland knows the realities of landscape restoration and that it is a partner that can be trusted over the long term. Twenty years of committed collaboration provides a realistic timeframe for people who know the land and want to see the benefits of that transformation for their children and the next generation of farmers.

Commonland activities and processes have helped the farmers of the Altiplano Estepario region to establish regenerative farming practices, including making swales (a sunken, shady marsh or swampy area), low-density rotational grazing, planting multiple complementary crops, creating windbreaks, and support ecological corridors and conservation. These practices retain soil and water in the landscape and enhance biodiversity. They also create markets for the organic produce from these farms ensuring that farmers receive higher prices. This creates opportunities for these farmers to continue investing in their farms and to witness the long-term impact of regenerative agriculture.[1] The main idea to note is the inspirational vision, which helps local people imagine a thriving future in their lands instead of seeing a dystopic vision of desertified lands that cannot sustain them with either produce or livelihoods. This is, of course, the return of inspiration, which then leads the way for the other returns such as the creation of jobs, of thriving people and communities, flourishing ecologies, and sustainable incomes.

Normalizing a better way of doing things

Both Willem and Simon left long-term, financially secure, and professionally rewarding jobs to start up the Commonland enterprise. But they were willing to take these risks in pursuit of their mission. From a GVV perspective, they were normalizing the risk dimension of regenerative entrepreneurship. At least to some degree, it is a normal part of entrepreneurship to take risks, even career-threatening ones, to follow the right path and expand the degrees of freedom for decision-making (Gentile, 2010). However, with a regenerative business a whole new set of risks are involved. First, because of the high stakes involved at the big scale of global sustainability regeneration is important work, among the most important work of our time. The Commonland founders were keenly aware of the implications of failure on this global scale. Second, at the organizational level, there are added market pressures because Commonland was not going to operate the way other development organizations did things. While a small number of other development organizations did take a landscape perspective, none did so over such a long timeframe or with such a holistic perspective on investment returns for such a broad spectrum of stakeholders. Third, at the personal level, like other business entrepreneurs, regenerative business leaders risk failure in following their dreams. But failure in developing truly sustainable economies affects generations of people and not just sole operators and regenerative entrepreneurs know this. While these factors combine to present a formidable set of risks, Willem and his co-founders wanted to situate Commonland as a model of how to normalize how things could be done differently.

Critically reflecting on what strategies will truly address those risks helps prioritize decisions and increases the tolerance for taking risks. There are severe risks in not pursuing regenerative sustainability goals. Doing nothing means following the Business-As-Usual (BAU) trajectories that are heightening catastrophic global risks to unacceptable levels (World Economic Forum, 2023). Taking these risks at the personal level of professional careers and financial security brings to public attention the need for shifting assumptions on what is possible, what is needed, and what should be the norm in the world or business and organizational behavior. The founders of Commonland reflected on such issues and asked questions about the implications of regenerative entrepreneuring for their own work and career aspirations. They reflected on the risks involved in pursuing regenerative work for their own professional careers and their contributions to a more sustainable world. They considered the risks of moving from the incremental to the transformative space in which Commonland wanted to operate.

Willem and Simon's ambitions to scale up Commonland's holistic development methods is realized in its global goal to benefit 1 billion people in 1,000 landscapes and transform 100 million hectares of restored land (an area twice the size of Spain) into thriving ecosystems and communities by 2040. Degraded land is land that has lost a significant degree of its natural resilience and productivity due to human-caused processes. About 50% of the world's terrestrial surface is classed as degraded. Degradation occurs when land rich in biodiversity loses many of its plants and animals, or when its topsoil is eroded or when its lakes and rivers get polluted with foreign chemicals and materials. Desertification (fertile land becoming desert), deforestation (excessive tree felling), savannization (rainforest becoming savannah), salinization (excessive salt levels), urbanization (natural landscapes into cities), kelp forest destruction, and eutrophication (excessive nutrient levels) are all examples of human-caused degradation processes.

Commonland works to reverse these processes through collaborating with local community organizations. Although they collaborate with many stakeholders in different organizational agreements, the foundation itself only has about 40 direct employees. Reaching their ambitious goals of restoration through landscape partnerships would be a significant achievement for such a small organization and would demonstrate to corporations the opportunities available to them for regenerative sustainability collaborations. Commonland works for this vision across many of the most challenging domains of social, ecological, and economic sustainability, including climate, biodiversity, water and land, community well-being and intergenerational resilience. To a greater or lesser extent, the many individuals and groups who get to know about this holistic vision have their assumptions of what is normal, what is possible and what is needed in building sustainable communities challenged. Challenging basic assumptions is an important step towards towards real change in management and farming practices.

Working with obstacles through "connection and love"

As an entrepreneur, Willem regularly encounters factors that can stymie Commonland's development. All entrepreneurs need to open new markets, find the right clients, recruit the best staff, overcome negative attitudes, and deal with bureaucracies. As a *regenerative* entrepreneur, he works with even more challenging barriers to achieving the organization's mission. There are several professional strategies that Willem employs to successfully innovate over the long term. One strategy is to reframe whatever hindrances he meets into everyday events that offer opportunities for moving forward. Willem regards the big and small challenges he faces every day not only as building resilience but also as enabling opportunities for deep growth and expressing core values. He says that "Values are everywhere" and that "most people share the values he expresses ... wherever they are from and whatever their political standpoint". Two of the foundational values for Willem are, as he says, "connection and love", where "love is caring about yourself and others." The allied goals of equality and unity for humanity are guiding principles for Willem, and this applies not only to the domain of values but to knowledge. He sees local and traditional knowledge and experience about the land just as valuable as the best scientific knowledge. All this knowledge comes from nature, and it guides and nurtures us.

> We all come from nature and are a part of nature - unity and holism – empathy for nature – if I am nature, then nurturing nature outside me, nurtures me and moves me towards ego-transcendence.

This sense of unity with nature is a key source of the fourth and most important of the 4 Returns framework that Commonland works with – inspiration. Inspiration was chosen by Willem as a neutral term to convey a sense of spirituality, positive potential, and reconnection that can speak to "multiple stakeholders". By placing inspiration, connection, and relationship at the center of the Commonland organizational values, Willem flips the typical model of how leaders and managers respond to the many challenges and demands facing contemporary businesses.

Normalizing regenerative investment

Commonland creates successful long-term projects by collaborating with partners who want to invest their money, time, passion, and labor in restoring and regenerating a region or landscape. Such collaborations do not come without struggle. It is extremely difficult to shift practices from the prevailing short-termism that dominates the agri-business sector and re-anchor new investments into a 20+-year investment perspective. This re-anchoring requires paradigmatic change that does not conform to the conventional assumptions of market capitalism. Willem and his Commonland colleagues quickly realized that it was essential that their partners share their long-term perspective and commitment to the 4 Returns Framework.

This need for vision and values partnering came to a head during the early development of Commonland when Willem was having crucial conversations with investors. A series of conversations were being held with a group of potential investors who were struggling with the idea of this very extended investment timeframe. They said that expecting investors to tolerate such a long wait for a return on their investment was a fantasy. Willem responded that it was the investors who were living in a dreamland if they thought ecological restoration and financial returns could come from any shorter investment horizon. He was aiming to normalize the long-term expectation for returns anchored in the conventional physical reality of how ecologies grow and flourish. Willem wanted to contrast the aspirational norm of patient capital with the conventional abnormal and unreal norms of current investment expectations and the accompanying long-term risks of thinking in the short to medium term.

The topic of investment is an area that frequently raises ethical dilemmas in the early life of an enterprise. Commonland needs funding to sustain its projects while they work toward financial independence via the revenues derived from revived landscapes. However, the organization is also careful not to dilute its mission by partnering with investors who do not share their regenerative vision and core values. In 2018, Willem was approached by a large corporation with a very substantial investment offer. The corporation was interested in collaborating with Commonland and in the process gain recognition for its sustainability strategy. This was a struggle for Willem. On the one hand, a sizeable investment could have a great deal of positive impact on the landscapes, but on the other hand it risked distorting the core values of Commonland and diluting its brand reputation with other stakeholders. The core operations of the would-be investor were not commensurate with regenerative goals. There was a real danger that the investment was a greenwashing exercise. Realizing that these types of misalignments were a part of being a transformative agent and having made decisions before where values trumped finances, Willem and his team decided to not accept the investment offer.

These kinds of conversations and decisions helped the investment community and other market players to understand Commonland's long-term investment cycle, its regenerative perspective, and the purpose of the 4 Returns Framework. Reframing what was taken to be the norm on investment returns did not magically remove the barriers that Willem often encountered when engaging with stakeholders. But this strategy of seeing things in a different light did help to navigate such issues with more freedom and insight. For example, these examples show how both Willem and Simon repeatedly practice having important conversations with key stakeholders so that enabling arguments can be tailored to overcome the most common rationalizations. In sharing with their various audiences, both Willem and Simon think about how they might persuasively express their vision and values, how they can draw on their own lived experiences, the arguments they can present that will powerfully convey their vision of optimizing economic, social, ecological, and inspirational returns.

Challenging false dichotomies

Willem and Commonland are both aware of the need to defuse apparent tensions and challenge false dichotomies; that is, the framing of choice into two equally unpleasant alternatives. Why not earn financial return *and* have a long-term investment horizon at the same time? What if these are not in opposition, but rather in a rare symbiosis? Investments in regenerative projects can be argued to bring financial security in the long term, while ensuring that the investment base for the three other returns are enhanced rather than depleted. Repeatedly engaging in these kinds of interactions with the market and it many players, Commonland is gradually gaining attention as an organization that normalizes the radical, that challenges financial assumptions, and that provides evidence for questioning the standard practices of investors. Reframing investment norms means that Willem and Commonland can enter honest and fruitful dialogues with the right kinds of investors. They can talk about the goals and priorities that matter to them rather than spending valuable time trying to persuade the wrong kinds of investors to come on board. This direct approach reinforces their sense of purpose and the strength of their values base. It also saves them from wasting time engaging with people and organizations that are not ready to take long-term committed action.

Normalizing regenerative education

As well as working with stakeholders in their own long-term partnership, Commonland also works with educational institutions, industry actors, and community members on the methods and impacts of the 4 Returns Framework. One example of this is the 4 Returns Platform, Commonland's education and resource-sharing platform. Spearheaded by Simon, the 4 Returns Academy and other educational initiatives disseminate insights and findings from their projects, supporting stakeholders to share experiences, impact data, and rich personal stories. Commonland and their partnering organizations monitor and evaluate what works in the landscapes with which they work. The knowledge they build together is utilized for mutual exchange and shared learning. Combining these insights from practice with academic concepts and engaging with transdisciplinary approaches they effectively scale their impact, normalizing the outlandish into something merely innovative.

The digital arena of the 4 Returns Community is building a joint body of knowledge and distributing it freely so that an insight generated in one landscape can be implemented swiftly in multiple similar locations or communicated to pique the interest of the public. In this sense, Commonland is practicing a regenerative and "co-evolutionary" form of sustainability that Landrum describes as "developing a mutually enhancing and beneficial relationship of balance, harmony, and synergy as an equal and contributing part of nature" (Landrum, 2018, p. 302). In the words of Commonland's mission: "making the 4 returns the new norm".

Insights

Embedded priorities

Something that becomes very apparent when examining the work of Commonland is how they subordinate the socio-economic and inspirational returns to the realities and overarching laws of nature. While operating in a way that respects the needs of financial capital, they do not allow it to set the agenda for the others. But it is also the case that regenerative entrepreneurship is not a philanthropic enterprise. It is a novel form of entrepreneurship that embeds financial returns within social returns while social returns are embedded in a natural environment that generates hope or inspiration for the future. This resonates with the embedded model of sustainability put forward by Kurucz, Colbert, and Marcus (2014), Griggs et al. (2013) and Edwards (2021).

Organizational voice

While Giving Voice to Values is most often applied to the individual and how they address ethical dilemmas, what Commonland shows us is that it can be just as applicable to the organizational level. Commonland was built upon the values of Willem and his partners, but in the process of maintaining and developing the organization, Commonland itself has become a vehicle for voicing values. For better or worse, organizations are something other than the individuals, technologies, and spatial domains that constitute them. That something extra is created and reproduced in the communications, structures, cultures, and values that go beyond any aggregate of individual persons. Commonland, as an organization, is expressing its core values in its mission and operations and in so doing is incrementally increasing the opportunity for other organizations to express their regenerative ideals.

Inspirational returns

Commonland uses the language of risk and returns to align the interests of different stakeholders. Of course, with entrepreneurial ventures comes a natural dimension of risk, not least when venturing into the uncharted territory of twenty-year investment periods. What enables entrepreneurs like Willem and Simon to persuade others to commit, to envision, and to make brave choices for the sake of regenerating socio-ecological systems is the inspiration they receive from being involved in this work. The inspirational returns lie at the heart of their enterprise. Inspirational returns energize the Commonland team and inspire the curiosity and commitment of their partners.

Normalizing the exceptional

Commonland's purpose is to regenerate large social ecological landscapes (above 100,000 hectares) and, more than this, to inspire other organizations, governments, financial institutions, and entrepreneurs to move into this opportunity. This is not a standard issue for organizational purpose, but, given the increasingly degraded state of the global biosphere, it is one that should be. With organizations such as Commonland building bridges between the exceptional and the normal, more people will find their way into this type of work and regenerative efforts will themselves become normalized within society. The earlier this social tipping point occurs (Otto et al., 2020), the greater the chances of becoming a sustainable society within a "safe and just operating space for humanity" (Raworth, 2017). Providing inspiration through the creation of flourishing human and ecological regions should be the default position of our economic systems and the organizations that constitute them. One particularly interesting strategy that Willem uses to communicate this at the individual level is to try, as he says, to "open the indigenous perspective within each individual", that is, to speak to the values that resonate with homeland, belongingness to country and to the territory in which we have grown up. Willem says, "if this resonates, you can have conversations from a whole different place". Normalizing these kinds of personal emotions and identities enables the regenerative and entrepreneurial task of engaging with deep sustainability values in organizational settings. Without such deep engagement it is not likely that the level of transformation of agricultural regions and communities that Commonland aims for could take place.

Extractive and regenerative responses to organizational tensions

The Commonland case highlights the distinction between extractive and regenerative responses to business environment pressures. While all organizations face tensions and paradoxes in achieving their goals, extractive business place the priority on financial objectives and consequently interpret social and environmental tensions as "costs" to be minimized or as "resources" to be utilized. From the perspective of the extractive business,[2] where the purpose is to extract as much financial value from the business as possible, factors that draw attention and resource away from profit maximization are sources of demand, tension, and pressure that need to be avoided, minimized, or neutralized in some way. Community interest demands, regulatory requirements, public environmental concerns, and increasingly stringent compliance standards are regarded as costs or demands that draw management away from the conventional business task of making profits. The result of this in many businesses is that managers feel themselves under immense pressure to respond to issues they see as peripheral to their core business function of generating revenue. A fragmented response results that refocuses on financial priorities, while simultaneously 'managing' non-pecuniary responsibilities and expectations. This fragmented response to business environment pressures can push many organizational decision-makers into 'hunkering down' and trade-off mentalities that focus on the business case while minimizing the "competing logics" of environmental and social demands. An extractive mindset results that seeks to focus values on the profit-making goals of the business. In contrast, a values-based, regenerative response reframes these demands and pressures as opportunities for expressing core values. Commonland exemplifies this regenerative response, in that multiple pressures are taken as opportunities for the voicing of values and the alignment of economic and social-ecological goals, strategies, and performance (see Figure 4.1).

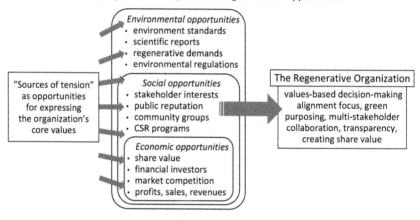

Figure 4.1 Extractive (a) and regenerative (b) responses to organizational demands.

Case questions

1. Commonland is a foundation that works toward regenerative purposes. Why is it that foundations are a good structure for for-purpose enterprises?

2. Why is it that Commonland can operate on such a long-term investment cycle of 20 years?

3. What role did the founders' early life experiences play in building the values of Commonland?

4. Why and how are the goals and purposes of Commonland becoming a more normal aspect of new business enterprises?
5. What role does the 4 Returns Framework play in Commonland's organizational purpose?
6. Why does the investment return of inspiration play such a key role in Commonland projects?

Workshop exercises

In this section, two exercises are outlined. One focuses on creative opportunities for imagining positive futures and the other normalizes the presence of voicing values in our own lives. These exercises are intended to open discussion and reflection on the GVV Pillar that has been the focus of this chapter – normalizing ethical dilemmas and opportunities. Normalization is about realizing that encountering ethical dilemmas and opportunities in the workplace is common. Therefore, it is important to prepare ourselves for effectively expressing our values.

Workshop Exercise 1   "What if? Yes and ..."

Regeneration is a call to action, a call to be the change we want to see in the world. It is a call to be courageous and creative, to take risks and to follow our hearts.

– Vandana Shiva

Articulate the challenge: In this exercise, you will explore the process of imagining regenerative business ventures and to challenge the tendency to seek out the problems of sustainable business development.

Time: 45–60 minutes

Purpose of the exercise: This exercise allows participants to think about regenerative entrepreneuring through playfully creating a story about a future business venture. Participants will role play regenerative entrepreneurs and skeptical investors. By participating in this exercise, we hone not only our capacity for imagination and creativity but also our competency for communicating that vision to others.

What does this exercise make possible? Speaking out our vision makes it real. We can also practice different ways to phrase our ideas, adjust our arguments and find our preferred styles. This builds confidence and skill for voicing our values.

Keywords: Vision exercise, *Improv* methodology, What if?

1. **Materials and spaces:** Facilitators will need a physical or digital space to gather as a group and as pairs. Participants need something to write on. It can be helpful to show appropriate visual aids which can either be shared on a screen or drawn simply.

2. **Group participation and configuration:** Participants are active in all the steps except when instructions are given. This is learning by doing. It is encouraged that everyone actively participates.

3. **Sequence of Steps and Time Allocation:**

   Step 1: Imagining a regenerative business venture (20 minutes). The first step is "What if? Yes and ..." exercise, commonly used in 'improv theater' classes. It allows creativity and playfulness to collaboratively build a story.

   • Divide the class into groups of 6. 4 students actively engage in the "What if? Yes and ..." exercise and 2 act as observers. The "What if? Yes and ..." exercise run as follows:

   • Participants imagine a regenerative scene 20 years in the future. It can be helpful to frame this vision with the 4 returns of inspirational, natural, social capital, and financial capital. For example, set the scene of needing to restore coral reefs, or build community resilience in developing regions or combat desertification. For example:

   Facilitator 1: *What if ... we formed a start-up to regenerate the coral reefs in Indonesia.* Follow up with giving the first "Yes and" response:

   Facilitator 2: "*Yes and — people would be moving back to abandoned coastal areas to go diving and see vibrant, diverse marine life.*"

   You then invite the group members to build on the vision by saying something like: Participant 1: "*Yes and - the local people create businesses like fishing and diving.*"

   You can go back and forth for a few rounds:

   Participant 2: "*Yes and — local podcasters got inspired to do a series on marine regeneration, which now has been heard by thousands of people.*"

> Participant 3: *"Yes and – this inspired other coastal areas to regenerate local reefs."*
>
> Participant 4: *"Yes and – this inspired governments to proclaim new marine parks."*

Tell participants to speak out the first ideas that come to mind. The rules are simply to start each round with "Yes, and …". This creates a spiral of imaginative possibilities. You might try doing several "Yes, and what if …" rounds starting with different scenarios.

As the process continues the observers make notes to capture the story and additional observations about the mood, the level of involvement, what worked and what did not.

Step 2: Note sharing – 10 minutes

The observers share their notes and discuss the regenerative scenario.

Step 3: Enabling arguments – 10 minutes.

Participants reflect on the gap between current reality and their scenario vision. What are the biggest challenges or obstacles to achieving this vision? How can this vision be communicated to sceptics who may not share the participants' values or beliefs? What arguments might the sceptics say to imply that it is impossible? Participants write down their best enabling suggestions to persuade the sceptics and counter their objections – 10 minutes.

Step 4: Meeting the investor – 10 minutes

Divide your groups into 3 pairs. Each pair consists of a regenerative entrepreneur and an investor. The regenerators start by sharing their vision (2 mins). The investors then produce their inhibiting arguments, saying why it will be just too risky and will not work. They give just one inhibiting point at a time. The regenerators respond to each critique with enabling arguments. The goal is to try to use the arguments written down in Step 3 to respond to the critiques by the sceptics. For both regenerators and investors, this is a kind of role play where they are asked to not be themselves, but only the roles of regenerator or sceptic. After 5 minutes, the roles are reversed.

Step 5: Returning to the class – 10 minutes

Open a reflective class discussion by inviting participants to share how it felt to do the exercise. What surprised them? What was challenging? What would they have done differently a second time around? Lastly, ask them to reflect on what insights this experience gives them for future real-world conversations. Connect it back to living and working as a regenerative entrepreneur.

4. **Tips and Traps**: Make sure participants do not feel that they are being graded on their performance. The exercise is meant for their benefit, and they should focus on having fun with it. Be clear in your instructions so that you avoid pairs spending time on the question: "What were we supposed to do?" As the facilitator you can potentially provide a batch of suggestions for future regenerated scenarios if you imagine this might be a struggle for participants.

5. **Variations**: You can do another exercise by just using step 2 – travelling to the future, either with the improv method in this exercise or simply by writing their vision down. This can be followed by individual participants envisioning how they see themselves contributing to that future reality This exercise is less interactive, but it is a useful way to practice manifestating and normalizing a regenerative future.

6. **Suggested extension materials**: reading, watching, podcasts, videos, articles, etc., to extend the participants' experience and learning.
   - 2040 (movie) – https://theregenerators.org/2040/
   - The natural step (framework) – https://thenaturalstep.org/
   - From What is to What if (book) – https://www.robhopkins.net/the-book/

Workshop Exercise 2   Regenerative Stories

Regeneration is the means by which enlightened, disruptive innovation happens.

– Carol Sandford

This exercise helps students to gain familiarity with regenerativity and to discover some of the innovations that regenerative businesses cases make possible.

Articulate the challenge: How can you develop a fine-grained understanding of organizational regenerativity? In this research exercise you will get an opportunity to learn how to do that.

Time: 50 minutes

Purpose of the exercise: The purpose of this exercise is to illustrate that regenerativity, either as a business or as a professional career, is becoming the norm.

What does this exercise make possible? By completing this quick exercise participants shine a light on their expectations about what business and professional possibilities exist in the regenerative sustainability field.

Structure of exercise: The exercise can be done by two people or more. It includes several steps of written reflections and sharing with a partner.

1. **Opening invitation**: This exercise requires active participation and personal reflection; therefore, it is important to set an expectancy of discovery and collaboration.

2. **Materials and spaces**: This exercise involves internet-based research, and the collaboration can be done onsite, online or hybrid.

3. **Sequence of steps and time allocation**:

   Step 1: In pairs or threes, find five organizational cases through online research that promote themselves as being regenerative. Drawing on as much material as possible, describe the organizations, ownership model, their industries and operations, mission/vision/purpose, strategies, and stakeholders.

   Step 2: Evaluate the actual level of generativity (e.g., high, moderate, or low) of each organization based on the criteria in Chapter 1. These are: i) restorative impact, ii) recognizes interdependency, iii) captures real value, iv) fosters imagination, v) supports empowerment, vi) utilizes technology and nature-based solutions, and vii) intergenerational planning.

   Step 3: Write up your findings for each case using the regenerativity criteria or the SOAR Analysis (Strengths, Opportunities, Aspirations and Results).

Tips and Traps: Ensure that groups do not pick the same organizations. The exercise might also be adapted to evaluate Commonland projects. These include Baviaanskloof DevCo, Grounded, La Almendrehesa, Habitat, AlVelAl Foods, La Sabina Milenaria, Wide Open Agriculture, Dirty Clean Food, Noongar Land Enterprise Group, Wilder Land, Aardpeer, and Boeren van Amstel (there are websites dedicated to each of these projects).

Variations: The exercise can be done as a set project or as an in-class activity.

Suggested extension materials: A pre-exercise could be to discuss the criteria and develop information-based indicators for each of them.

Notes

1 There are many details available on the internet on the Altiplano Estepario project and free online courses are available on regenerative farming and Commonland projects. For more information see: The 4 Returns website and Rotterdam School of Management – Commonland Case Study – https://www.rsm.nl/cdc/multimedia-cases/commonland/

2 See section entitled "Regenerative Entrepreneurs and the Extractive Economy" in Chapter 3.

References

Brovkin, V., Brook, E., Williams, J. W., Bathiany, S., Lenton, T. M., Barton, M., ... Yu, Z. (2021). Past abrupt changes, tipping points and cascading impacts in the Earth system. *Nature Geoscience, 14*(8), 550–558. doi:10.1038/s41561-021-00790-5

Buldyrev, S. V., Parshani, R., Paul, G., Stanley, H. E., & Havlin, S. (2010). Catastrophic cascade of failures in interdependent networks. *Nature, 464*(7291), 1025–1028. http://www.nature.com/nature/journal/v464/n7291/suppinfo/nature08932_S1.html

Commonland. (2022). *Building a New Balance between Ecology, Economics and Hope.* Retrieved from https://www.commonland.com/

Dudley, N., Baker, C., Chatterton, P., Ferwerda, W., Gutierrez, V., & Madgwick, J. (2021). *The 4 Returns Framework for Landscape Restoration.* Amsterdam, The Netherlands.

Edwards, M. G. (2021). The growth paradox, sustainable development, and business strategy. *Business Strategy and the Environment, 30*(7), 3079–3094. doi:10.1002/bse.2790

Ferwerda, W. (2015). *4 Returns, 3 Zones, 20 Years: A Holistic Framework for Ecological Restoration by People and Business for Next Generations*. Rotterdam: People and Business for Next Generations, Rotterdam School of Management, IUCN-CEM, Commonland.

Folke, C., Jansson, Å., Rockström, J., Olsson, P., Carpenter, S., Chapin, F. S. III, ... Westley, F. (2011). Reconnecting to the biosphere. *Ambio, 40*(7), 719–738. doi:10.1007/s13280-011-0184-y

Gentile, M. C. (2010). *Giving Voice to Values: How to Speak Your Mind When You Know What's Right*. New Haven, CT: Yale University Press.

Griggs, D., Stafford-Smith, M., Gaffney, O., Rockstrom, J., Ohman, M. C., Shyamsundar, P., ... Noble, I. (2013). Sustainable development goals for people and planet. *Nature, 495*(7441), 305–307. doi:10.1038/495305a

Kurucz, E. C., Colbert, B. A., & Marcus, J. (2014). Sustainability as a provocation to rethink management education: Building a progressive educative practice. *Management Learning, 45*(4), 437–457.

Landrum, N. E. (2018). Stages of corporate sustainability: Integrating the strong sustainability worldview. *Organization & Environment, 31*(4), 287–313. doi:10.1177/1086026617717456

Lenton, T. M., Rockström, J., Gaffney, O., Rahmstorf, S., Richardson, K., Steffen, W., & Schellnhuber, H. J. (2019). Climate tipping points – Too risky to bet against. *Nature, 575*, 592–595.

Moolenaar, S. W., van Tulder, R., Thorsson, J., Favretto, N., Arnalds, Ó., Aradottir, A. L., & Kennedy, S. (2023). *Commonland Case Study: Spain – A Business Approach to Sustainable Landscape Restoration*. Retrieved from https://fr.coursera.org/lecture/landscape-restoration-sustainable-development/commonland-case-study-spain-q1uDw

Otto, I. M., Donges, J. F., Cremades, R., Bhowmik, A., Hewitt, R. J., Lucht, W., ... Schellnhuber, H. J. (2020). Social tipping dynamics for stabilizing Earth's climate by 2050. *Proceedings of the National Academy of Sciences, 117*(5), 2354. doi:10.1073/pnas.1900577117

Raworth, K. (2017). *Doughnut Economics: Seven Ways to Think Like a 21st-Century Economist*. London: Chelsea Green Publishing.

World Economic Forum (Ed.) (2023). *Global Risks 2023: Insight Report* (18th ed.). Geneva: WEF.

5

THE MOST PRECIOUS METAL ON EARTH

This case presents the social innovation Humanium Metal (HM) and two entrepreneurs who were intimately involved in the founding and development of the HM venture. The case materials were collated from online sources and from interviews with two IM entrepreneurs Simon, the Business and Innovation Manager, and Jacqueline, the Program and Advocacy Lead. HM is a business initiative of the parent organization, Individuell Människohjälp (IM *Swedish Development Partner*), a Swedish international development organization. From our analysis of these sources, insights are developed into how the leaders overcome obstacles to express their core values in powerful and persuasive ways. The case provides insights into the alignment between personal commitment and organizational purpose and mission. Some workshop exercises intended to explore this topic of aligning individual and collective purpose follow at the end of the chapter.

DOI: 10.4324/9781003330660-5

THE CASE OF HUMANIUM METAL IN BRIEF

Organization name: Humanium Metal
Year of founding: 2016
Website: https://humanium-metal.com/
Type of organization: A not-for-profit subsidiary of the not-for-profit international development Individuell Människohjälp (*IM Swedish Development Partner*),
Purpose/mission of organization: Humanium Metal (HM) addresses gun violence by transforming seized and destroyed illegal firearms into a metal called "Humanium". Humanium is used to create high-quality products with the aim of raising awareness about gun violence and generating funds to development communities in regions affected by gun violence. HM recycles violence into beauty as an example of innovation that combines social impact, regenerative sustainability with economic renewal.
Industry/community sector: International development and human rights
Services: HM offers services that enable the transformation of gun metal into designed personal products. These services include firearm collection and destruction, metal production, international collaborations, gun violence awareness and advocacy, peace and justice promotion, product design, and production and sales.
Locations: HM has operations in Sweden, El Salvador, Zambia and the USA
Impact and achievements: Sales from HM products amounted to US$1,613,000 in 2021. HM has been awarded or nominated for several international prizes: the Grand Prix for Innovation at the Cannes Festival for Creativity, 2017; Fast Company's World Changing Ideas Awards, 2018; nominated for the Billion Acts of Peace Award, 2021. HM has become "a breeding ground for social change in El Salvador" (Esmeralda Mejia – HM volunteer and peace activist).

The most precious metal on Earth – Humanium Metal

Humanium Metal is a social business innovation launched by its parent organization, Individuell Människohjälp (IM *Swedish Development Partner*), a Swedish international development organization. IM works to achieve poverty elimination, social inclusion, and sustainability. It was founded in 1938 by the Swedish social entrepreneur and politician Britta Holmström as a response to the growing humanitarian crisis in Europe. IM grew rapidly during and immediately after World War II and provided support for the many refugees and victims of that tumultuous conflict. Since this time, the work of IM has concentrated on collaborative projects and the individual worth of every person as a counterweight to the oppression and violence that often results from ideological conflict and systemic corruption. IM works with all levels of society to create social, economic, and environmental initiatives that target the United Nations Sustainable Development Goals (SDGs). Currently, IM has established operations in many regions of the world, including Central America, the Middle East, South Asia, and Southern Africa.

Humanium Metal (HM) is a social business enterprise initiated by IM. The initial impetus for the HM start-up came from IM's Peter Brune. HM's mission is to reduce gun violence by recycling weapons into metal products and using the revenues for peace building and justice programs. The purpose of HM is to:

> [E]mpower and support survivors of violence, giving them strength, knowledge, and confidence in themselves to stand up against violence. Youths reclaim public spaces as violence-free zones and mobilize their communities to unite against violence.
>
> (Humanium Metal, 2020)

In effect, HM's mission is to transform violence into beauty, to recycle gun metal into something that communicates peace through aesthetics and artistic design. Gun violence is a destructive and terrorizing force in both advanced and impoverished countries. Gang warfare, illegal militias, and organized crime syndicates can cause immense harm in communities where guns are easily available. Sometimes governments implement weapons destruction programs, gun moratoriums and seizure programs in affected regions and stockpile the gathered weapons. HM breaks down these stockpiles of weapons, extracts the metal (called Humanium Metal), and transforms it into metal ingots and metal powder. It then engages with businesses, entrepreneurs, designers, and artists to develop products such as watches, jewelry, machines, and works of art. HM products are designed and marketed as "commodities for peace" so that customers are informed of the HM mission and can feel that they are contributing to its mission.

HM was first produced in 2016 in El Salvador, using firearms seized by the Salvadoran government. El Salvador was chosen as a pilot region for the business, as the country is heavily affected by extreme levels of armed violence. There is also dedicated support at many levels of society to address this issue to achieve inclusive socio-economic development in the region. In 2018 HM expanded further into Zambia and the United States of America. Figure 5.1 outlines the HM circular business model. The most common method for producing HM is through government seizure programs. Illegal firearms are "destroyed", and the metal melted down and turned into ingots, wire, or pellets. The metal is sent to Sweden and reduced to powder that can be more easily used in the 3D printing production of metal products. Examples of HM products that use the metal in their manufacturing process include watches, pens, spinning tops, buttons, bracelets, and headphones.

The income generated is re-invested into communities affected by gun violence and so aims to break the vicious cycle of violence and poverty. Host community activities funded from the business's profits include supporting survivors of armed violence with income generation, empowering communities to reclaim public spaces as violence-free zones, empowering youths to choose violence-free paths, and supporting communities to advocate for legislation that prevents gun violence. The revenues flowing

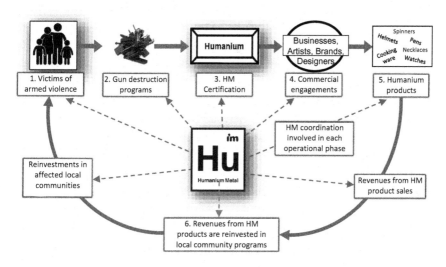

Figure 5.1 Humanium Metal's circular business model.

from the overall sale of HM products have exceeded US$5 million since the beginning of the enterprise. The income generated for societal change has now exceeded US$1.2 million with all this money being channeled to HM community partners. The business activity of upcycling a commodity used for violence and killing into consumable goods for peace creates a platform for a global movement for peace and security.

The entrepreneurs

Jacqueline Duerre – Program and advocacy lead for HM

Jacqueline Duerre is the Program and Advocacy Lead for HM, and the venture plays a significant role in her life. She identifies strongly with the purpose of the IM organization and the HM enterprise. This is particularly the case for the circular sustainability, equity, anti-racist, and pro-feminist values that are non-debatable values for Jacqueline and for the IM parent organization. Jacqueline grew up in a very multicultural Berlin in the period following the unification of Germany. She developed a keen sense of human rights, universal values, and cosmopolitan identity while growing up in a family that had been impacted by the turbulent events of World War II and the Cold War. Powerful and horrific stories of the war were ever-present in her childhood and, in later life, the feeling of wanting to contribute from her position of privilege and good luck became a big motivation. Growing up in West Berlin, Jacqueline absorbed a powerful sense of multiculturalism and cosmopolitanism that characterized the youth culture of the city. But there was also the dark side of history that was also built into her surroundings. For example, most of her friends, although born in Germany, were from diverse cultural backgrounds, and were denied German citizenship because they were not born into German families. Jacqueline studied social sciences and after graduating she worked in jobs that did not fully satisfy her professional aspirations. Equipped with her motivation to 'give back' and a love of travelling and experiencing diverse cultures, Jacqueline looked for a position in international development and in 2019 she took up the job with IM to set up the first full pilot of the HM enterprise.

The core purpose of HM is to work on changing the system that perpetuates communal violence and to target preventative and regenerative interventions rather than adopting a reactive approach. The HM approach is regenerative because it meets many of the definitive criteria for regenerativity outlined in Chapter 1. It is positively restorative of human communities in that it builds their economic, social, and environmental resilience. It creates "real value" (Sternad, Kennelly, & Bradley, 2016) in that it rebuilds long-term human relationships, social innovation, and local leadership. It is transformative in that it radically shifts mindsets from the problem of violence to the opportunity for social creativity. It empowers participation through rebuilding security, community confidence, and consumer awareness. It innovates for circularity and upcycling rather than adopting standard developmental mentalities. Humanium Metal (HM) is regenerative in that it transforms death into life, community violence into community emancipation, human despair into art and beauty.

All these elements of the HM model reflect Jacqueline's values and her passion for justice, equality, and integrity. This alignment between organizational purpose and her personal values was a guiding factor in Jacqueline's choice to work for IM and to be involved in the setting up of HM. Looking at the big picture, Jacqueline is motivated by her passion for justice given some of the global problems of unequal access to opportunities and the injustice that is apparent for many people living in both poor and rich countries. The lack of financial equality is one of several unfair disadvantages that Jacqueline saw people subjected to. There was also personal power, education, gender equality, access to employment, and many other areas of life that, for no good reason, were available to some and not to others. These issues impacted on her personal sense of morality and on her emotions already as a child.

Jacqueline feels that she is a pragmatic person who has her ideals but also a sense of professional pragmatism. It is important to have ideals to inform your vision and purpose, but you also need to connect with the other person and make it easy for them. She feels that sometimes she silences herself for pragmatic reasons and compromises on processes but not on the values themselves. She realistically knows that sometimes you need to choose the time, the place, and the people before acting on your concerns. She says we need to work with each other and, when necessary, reach compromises on certain points but compromising on the big issues and on core values is not an option.

Simon Marke Gran – Business and innovation lead

Simon Marke Gran has been working with HM since 2016, focusing on developing the metal and the product lines. In previous positions Simon worked in management roles, including business development and innovation, public communications, and partnership development. Much of his current work involves the development of business ideas and collaborations with artists and designers and with researchers from educational institutions. Simon has been heavily engaged with HM and is committed to the enterprise as an expression of both his personal and professional purpose. His commitment to the core goals of HM – ending gun violence and community development – is strong and he feels that it informs his sense of identity and reaffirms his self-image of wanting to be contribute to something bigger than his own personal world of concerns. He feels that HM is "an expression of who I am as a person". Because HM has such a powerful and easily communicated purpose, corporate brands and quality businesses want to be involved. But there is also the real risk of companies wanting to be involved for greenwashing purposes. Consequently, Simon's alignment of personal and organizational identity also motivates his sense of loyalty and protection of the HM 'brand'. Consequently, he finds that discretion and clear judgment need to be exercised in HM collaborations at every point in the value network.

Because Simon comes from a corporate background, he knows the importance of image and branding, but also that collaborations need to go well beyond that. For example, he develops relationships with corporate partners who are interested in the social investment dimension of the project and not just the "guns into jewelry" image. Simon knows that HM has a strong brand, but he wants to ensure it goes beyond this simple image and to publicly promote HM's social focus on developing communities, investing in young people, and restorative justice and communicating all that with business partners. The right partner must be selected to ensure that HM can maximize the communication of how connected the world really is and how there is always the possibility of making a real difference in the communities it works in.

Simon finds great professional fulfilment in supporting communities and working with youth to provide local opportunities for work and other activities. He feels that his work contributes to creating a global movement for peace and that customers' awareness about human rights and sense of connection with less privileged communities is raised through purchasing HM products. The HM product gives customers a chance to voice their values and connect with marginalized communities in a positive way. As Simon puts it:

> HM inspires hope in our human capacity to support each other and transform towards something better. To help us be more humane.

From Simon's perspective, HM is not only about reducing gun violence but also about addressing a multiplicity of factors that cause the breakdown of community life. There is a long history of exploitation and economic and political colonization behind the community unrest and gang violence that pervades countries like those in Central America. Simon feels that the HM enterprise can make a real difference to many communities throughout this region and other parts of the world, and redress some of the factors that cause these problems.

Simon places great value on his professional integrity and accountability. Before his work with HM, he had been working in the mainstream finance sector in Hong Kong, and in Switzerland. Throughout his working life, being true to his values and keeping aware of social issues and environmental challenges had always been a big part of Simon's life. However, as he spent more years working in the financial investment industry, he began to feel that he was putting more distance between his current work and where he wanted to be. He felt he was "falling away from the real me". When he saw this, he changed direction and took up the business and innovation lead position with the HM start-up and he knows this was the right decision.

Integrity for Simon means holding and expressing the same set of core values at home, at work, and wherever he might be. For example, his sense of human solidarity is not something to be separated from his professional identity and responsibilities. He feels a sense of loyalty and commitment to the people that are affected by gun violence, the "right holders", the ones who have the right to speak up about gun violence. It can be frustrating to be so involved and committed because there are constraints on what can be achieved. But these constraints also call for ingenuity and innovation. Simon appreciates HM's ambition to have global impact, but he also knows that this can be slow in coming.

Simon describes himself as a pragmatic idealist; that is, someone who prioritizes organizational values and moral commitments while at the same time making sure he looks after himself, his colleagues, and stakeholder partners in practical ways. He is a risk-taker in the pursuit of big ideals, but this does not mean all pragmatic calculations go out the window. Pragmatists like Simon tend to develop and apply strategies to deal with an ethical dilemma according to the situation. He likes to find allies who are experts for the requirements of the situation because they simply speak their mind and provide useful knowledge that feeds into the decision-making process. Similarly, his preferred way of communicating when faced with an ethical problem or opportunity will depend on the situation. He feels the most important strengths he brings into the workplace are his clear focus on values-based decision-making but this can also bring tensions. For example, holding firmly to core values can produce conflict when personal priorities clash. At such times, Simon finds that searching for a balance and digging deeper into the underlying motivations to find alignments can diplomatically resolve such issues. Taking entrepreneurial risks is exactly one such topic that can cause conflict. When HM was just getting off the ground there was a time when financial risks were putting pressure on commitments to community stakeholders. There were tensions between the need to secure financial funding and meeting commitments of investment into the communities we had promised to support. Those tensions were real because as Simon puts it, "everything that we do has not been done before". But openly discussing these issues enabled HM to find innovative ways forward that aligned core values and reinforced core commitments.

While centers of authority and leadership are important, they can also stifle innovation and Simon finds it essential to encourage a work climate of questioning and curiosity. Searching for useful questions can be a wonderful way to open new possibilities. When encountering ethical dilemmas, Simon feels that it is crucial to confidently voice your values within the organization and that this needs to be much more widely discussed and researched. This confidentiality can only occur in an environment of trust. Working at the forefront of social innovation and change requires generous levels of trust and confiding in colleagues to seek their advice and support is one way an organization can nurture trust as a natural part of work relationships.

The HM business model and circularity

There has been a terrible parade of contributing factors to the ongoing community violence that so harms local community life. The postcolonial impact of institutionalized violence, decades of government neglect, lack of economic stability, geopolitical trickery, violent foreign intervention, political instability, the ready availability of firearms and, more recently, the destabilizing effects of climate change combine to produce a deadly cocktail of destabilizing intimidation and violence. Even amid all this, however, communities are still full of life and demonstrating resilience to partner with local and international agencies to seek solutions. Breaking the cycle of violence with the recycling of gun metal, however, challenges the established power order and can therefore upset the organized centers of corrupt political and gang power. But the benefits are so transformative that local groups, affected families, courageous individuals, and community leaders are willing to take the risks and work with HM to create the social benefits that flow from the HM business model. This is a powerful form of social regenerativity. Figure 5.1 shows the circular nature of the HM business model, and the multiple stakeholders are intimately involved in the social-ecological value network[1] of the HM business model. It is more apt to speak of the HM business model as a spiral rather than as circle. HM is about changing the whole trajectory of gun violence in the communities it works in. It is about a spiral of virtue rather than a spiral into violence. Figure 5.1 shows that guns are transformed into resources and products for supporting communities – a virtuous spiral of violence into hope and human potential.

With her sensibility for justice and equity, Jacqueline finds it enriching to work with local stakeholders to support the HM business model of deep value creation. It is *deep* value that is being created here because it is not just economic but diverse varieties of social and environmental wealth that is produced. Deep value is especially evident when youth transform their lives and move from crime and violence into regenerative forms of livelihood. While regenerativity has typically been associated with greater levels of ambition in environmental sustainability, in the HM case it is social regenerativity that comes to the fore. It is not just the reduction of harm to human ecosystems that is being sought here, nor even the goal of zero harm, but a much more positive vision of lives lived for their true potential of educational developmental, cultural growth, and social maturation.

The notion of life cycle sustainability takes on special and profound meaning in the context of the HM circular business model. Take the case of David, a boy of twelve getting up early to go to work when, just as he stepped onto the street outside his family home, he was shot. No rhyme or reason to it; just pure, purposeless violence. The gun was there, the perpetrator's unknown story of abuse and violence was there, and David was left in the street hanging grimly onto his life. The gunshot had torn through his spinal cord and left David with paralysis in his lower body. With the support of his family and community and financial support from HM, David slowly recovered and went home to learn how to live with his wheelchair. But David has immense courage and spirit and soon began to work towards his dreams and put his entrepreneurial business skills to work. He sells street wares in the local towns from his wheelchair and is now saving money for his further education and business ventures. HM supports the victims of gun violence like David and his family. They provide funding, but also training and skills development to help families recover from violence and lead lives that they are proud of. All this requires creativity and determination, qualities that characterize all the HM staff.

Meeting ethical challenges

Both Jacqueline and Simon recognize that ethical challenges are a normal occurrence in their work. Knowing this helps them to be prepared with strategies that can resolve dilemmas or at least buy time so they can reflect on the matter at hand and do some background research. One challenge they sometimes face is working with stakeholders who, while being important players in the HM value network, are themselves centers of corruption in the communities in which they are operating. Local police forces can be particularly difficult in that their cooperation is needed and yet many of their members are part of the problem. In such situations, Simon and Jacqueline internally discuss issues such as how to go proceed, what their core values are, and "where is our red line?" In some instances, there are clear standards and lines not to be crossed; in others, however, some innovation and workarounds are needed. There is no standard answer; it is very context-based. Jacqueline remarked that "One thing that is always prioritized is that everyone involved in the project, especially our partners and right holders that live in the country, have to be safe at all points". To ensure this safety HM works more on a municipal or city level rather than a national level. At the municipal level, they can have more control and integration within local communities rather than being dependent on the government bureaucracies.

Jacqueline thinks that it makes a massive difference to have a well-defined purpose when facing ethical dilemmas or situations where solutions need to be improvised. She makes sure that she discusses any such dilemmas with their colleagues in the IM organization. Both Jacqueline and Simon always come back to the parent organization's (IM) values when formulating strategy. "This is what we stand for"; "This is what we lean on when faced with ethical dilemmas".

On a more personal level, Jacqueline described a situation that arose soon after the first full piloting of the HM project. In the beginning HM was like a start-up where everything had to be done at the same time. It was a time of huge energy and activity. Everything had gone very well, and HM delivered its first significant financial returns. The idea was that HM would eventually be financially independent from IM and follow a circularity model, financially as well as materially. The reason for the existence of HM was to raise money from the sales of its metal and products and for those revenues to be reinvested back into civil society, back into the neighborhoods where the gun metal came from. IM had given assurances to the El Salvadorian government that this investment of HM proceeds would take place. But there was a problem with the initial round of funding. The HM project had been running for some time, and Jacqueline was employed and working full-time with the start-up. IM had invested a lot into the start-up enterprise. IM had assurances that a grant would be awarded from the Swedish government but, because of political changes at that time, it was unclear if they would ever receive that grant and the HM start-up was in danger of going into significant debt. By this time, the first sale of metal had already taken place and IM had these proceeds available from HM commercial sales. The guns had been collected, the metal recycled and smelted into products and the beautiful jewelry and art pieces had been sold to provide the first intake of cash.

There were discussions on whether the money raised from the initial sales should be used to cover HM's operational costs or should it be invested, as promised, back into the communities where the guns came from. Jacqueline was at a meeting where this was being specifically discussed. The financial situation had triggered a discussion on the reinvestment question. Jacqueline said at the meeting that she wanted to work for IM and HM because of the innovative aspect of the circularity approach they were taking. Traditionally, international development is not regarded as an innovative sector and the HM initiative stood out from the pack because its entrepreneurial melding of sustainability, circularity, and social justice was so unique. This was one of the main reasons Jacqueline wanted to work with the organization. During the meeting Jacqueline said she did not want the job if this circular aspect of reinvestment did not take place, especially since assurances had already been given. She also expressed her strong view that it was even more important in this first full piloting of the start-up that a complete cycle of the scheme needed to be run to establish trust and faith in its viability. Although her own job could have been at risk, Jacqueline felt that establishing trust in the circularity of the process was vital, especially with the first receipt of revenues. Those first proceeds had to be reinvested back into the affected neighborhoods otherwise the trust of the other stakeholders in IM and the HM start-up would have been broken. The values of trust, loyalty, and honesty were central to this decision for Jacqueline. Senior leadership quickly decided that the proceeds from the HM sales must go back to El Salvador and be invested in the community programs there and IM injected additional funds until HM could stand on its own two feet.

This incident is notable for several reasons. First, it highlights the values-based decision making that is a characteristic of IM culture. More than this, however, it shows the commitment of the organization to a strong prioritization of values. Awareness of the importance of upholding trust and the resolute commitment to formally agreed arrangements were prioritized above financial concerns. It might be expected that a non-profit organization would always take this values-based approach but that would be to reduce the pressure on non-profit organizations to be fiscally responsible and accountable. IM, for example, needs to submit many financial reports every year to various auditing bodies and the pressure to demonstrate a strong financial performance is high. The episode also shows that Jacqueline is quick to express her values, even when she might come out the poorer for it. In this instance, however, it was clear that the leadership environment was one that supported her speaking honestly about her views. There was even an expectation that she would do so. The incident demonstrates that when a person skillfully expresses their views within a supported workplace environment even tough decisions can be resolved with minimal fuss and the reaffirmation of values provides a kind of cultural capacity building that strengthens the organization's ability to navigate its challenges with proven values and methods for expressing them.

One person, one family, one community at a time

One of the core values that guides HM and Simon and Jacqueline in their work is the practical impact on the lives of real people and the challenges they face in their communities. HM aims to build peaceful societies that can work towards sustainable development, and it does this by funding and supporting people, families, and communities in practical ways. The story of Wendy in El Salvador and the community Red de Sobrevivientes (Survivors Network) provide a powerful example of individuals and communities who have been affected by gun violence and, with HM support, continue to work for peace and for familial and community well-being.[2]

Wendy was a 16-year-old young woman in El Salvador when she was cut down by gunshot. But she transformed her life and her career options to become a lawyer and founder of a disability rights agency by the time she was 32. In 2004 Wendy was selling bread with a relative on a local street near her home. Two men approached them and, without a word, murdered her relative and shot Wendy five times. She collapsed and was barely alive but was rushed to the hospital by police. After several months fighting for her life and learning to live again Wendy began the long rehabilitation process of rebuilding that life began. Because of the paralysis she was in a wheelchair and battling with the physical and psychological implications of that. But this was not the worst of her struggles. During her recovery in hospital Wendy had initiated legal action against the perpetrators who she recognized and knew belonged to a local gang. The two men were arrested. Members of the gang came to the hospital and threatened to kill both her and her family if they did not withdraw the charges. With the support and direction of her family, Wendy withdrew all charges and the men were released. Such are the realities for communities living with extreme gun violence.

Then followed several years when Wendy learned to accept her new identity and live with a disability. Through HM, their partners and other community organizations, Wendy has gained access to rehabilitation services, education, and personal development support. One such agency that partners with HM is Red de Sobrevivientes. Red de Sobrevivientes is a network of gun violence survivors and people with disabilities in El Salvador and it promotes a human rights approach to the inclusion of people with disabilities in community. Jaqueline, Simon, and the other members of the

HM team with agencies like Red de Sobrevivientes to advance the rights, the security, and the future potential of individuals like Wendy, her family, and the community she lives in and works for. Today, Wendy is a single mum with two children and works as a lawyer. As a woman with a disability, she has challenged, and overcome, many significant social obstacles. Being a woman and having a profession with high status is itself a challenge in El Salvador. Wendy sees HM as an important initiative, not only to strengthen individuals affected by gun violence but also for the entire work of changing the culture of violence in El Salvador. HM supports many others like Wendy who have been affected by gun violence. Financial, educational, and social opportunities are made available for both personal and professional development. In this and many other ways, HM contributes to rebuilding communities affected by the horror of gun violence. Wendy says this rebuilding is a long and complicated process, but she knows that it is possible.

Strategies for dealing with ethical challenges

Ethical challenges as motivating opportunities

Stories like those of Wendy and David and their supporting community organizations show the power of change that can result from individual courage and commitment partnerships. However, while there is a strong alignment of values and goals for the key stakeholders in HM's value network, differences and potential conflicts will always arise. There is also the complex matter of the multiple goals that HM itself aims to achieve in areas such as environmental sustainability and financial performance. For example, one area that has been difficult for Jacqueline is the contentious issue of the environmental impact of the smelting of weapons. Turning the gun metal into something that can be of value for crafting high-quality jewelry is a costly and energy-rich process that consumes a lot of energy and produces copious amounts of greenhouse gas emissions. Even when alternative energy sources can be found, the environmental impact of the manufacturing, transportation, and packaging processes can be significant. Jacqueline works actively to minimize these aspects of the HM value networks and uses these constraints as motivation for further innovation. One aspect of her critical thinking capacities that she acquired in her adolescent years is this ability to think in contrarian and novel ways and this analytical eye serves her well in her work with HM. The occasional misalignment between environmental and social sustainability spurs her toward finding solutions. For example, both Simon and Jacqueline have been in conversation with key figures in the metal production process and experimented with alternative renewable energy sources, emissions reductions, and product innovation in the design and production process.

Preparation and 'pre-scripting'

Prior to important meetings or when they feel the need to reaffirm core understandings, Jacqueline and Simon practice a pre-scripting exercise where they discuss together the issues that could emerge in a specific meeting or, more generally, in everyday project management. They discuss the central objectives they might have for a meeting, think about the kinds of tactics other stakeholder might use when confronting some contentious topic, and assess how to present the core purposes and values that they see as relevant for an important presentation.

The prudent use of exercises like pre-scripting depends a lot on self-reflexivity and on a person's capacity for insight and self-knowledge.

Self-reflection and face-to-face

Jacqueline often takes a few moments to practice self-reflection about how societal norms and expectations affect her and our society. This helps her to understand her own reactions and preferences, and the behaviors and choices of other stakeholders and rightholders and how they respond to challenges. She has always used the inspiration of role models to help her in that process. When trying to resolve interpersonal disagreements and conflicts, she feels that face-to-face approaches work best for her. However, when it is important that a discussion be documented, she adopts email communications as a way of recording decisions that have been reached. When faced by an ethical dilemma in the future she thinks it's good to: find allies, "people that I can go to if I need motivation or just to like to complain a bit, have a rant, create a safe space", be self-reflective with a critical voice to check your assumptions, ask yourself is my stance right? To avoid making the same mistakes, it is important to learn from them and to build your capacity for applying that learning.

Finding trusted allies

As a natural part of doing her work, Jacqueline seeks out the opinions of others to discuss inherent risks and the common interests of stakeholders and rightholders. She looks for allies to find a supportive space where she can reflect on events and confide in others about her own hopes and doubts. In the process of finding allies, forums are explored where HM can advocate for its partners and contact potential allies. The powerful symbolism of the HM business model has created a platform to elevate the discussion of gun violence, which has not been adequately represented in international forums on disarmament, violence, or terrorism. The power of that symbolism has been recognized by the United Nations in their Permanent Disarmament Exhibition in New York when they included several HM products as part of that exhibition. HM utilizes its powerful business model to bring an innovative voice of advocacy to international forums on disarmament and gun violence. Working in this fashion supports the connection of allies and shared interests for violence prevention in actions such as working towards the UN Sustainable Development Goals (e.g., SDG 16 – Promote just, peaceful, and inclusive societies) and the UN Program of Action on Small Arms and Light Weapons.

Strategies for grasping opportunities

Enabling opportunities

It is important to recognize that ethical issues, let us call them ethical moments, occur frequently through the day. Whether they be dilemmas and problems or opportunities for achieving goals and purposes, they will arise at many points in a day's work. While most will be small in scale that does not mean they are unimportant. It is particularly interesting to note those ethical moments can also appear as positive opportunities for expressing values. That is as moments to grasp by expressing one's aspirations, creative ideas, and dreams. Jacqueline mentions times when, in contrast to raising a problem, an opportunity is made available for moving towards core goals or being creative and opening new avenues for engagement with stakeholders. Such times present opportunities for speaking up not to confront dilemmas but to initiate change. At times like these one's internal state, one's own capacity to grasp opportunities is called upon.

Jacqueline relates a time when she missed just such an opportunity. She and Simon were working with a new set of stakeholders in a new country, and they were excited to expand the HM enterprise into a new market. But there were problems raised by some of the key stakeholders about the need for different approaches to producing the Humanium Metal itself. They insisted that local industries needed to be involved in the part of the value network that took the gun metal and smelted it into Humanium ingots. There were some tense negotiations over this aspect of the new initiative and in the end the project did not proceed. Jacqueline feels that she did not speak up at certain critical moments to introduce ideas that could have resolved the stalemate. It was not a dilemma that brought about her silence; rather, it was the lack of recognition of an opportunity for creative involvement and leadership. She reflected on this later and knew that next time she would act differently, sit down with the stakeholders, and coordinate a process of innovation and collaborative planning rather than allow such an opportunity to slide by.

Insights

HM and the three pillars of regenerative sustainability

The HM enterprise and the entrepreneurs that lead and direct its activities portray the social sustainability side of regenerativity. Regenerativity has typically been presented in sustainability literature as having an environmental focus. This is not surprising given the heightened awareness and increasing urgency of environmental issues such as climate change, biodiversity loss, and impending tipping points in crucial Earth biophysical systems. HM, however, places its focus on regenerating human communities by removing weapons and reinvesting in neighborhood security, education, and employment. This is usefully seen as a social form of regenerative sustainability. Interestingly, IM, HM's parent organization, supports sustainable farming and community gardening programs in these same communities in order to improve food security, nutrition, and skill development. The aim is to have regenerative impacts on both human and ecological communities. HM presents an interesting case where the three pillars of sustainability – the economic, the social, and the environment – are each treated from a regenerative perspective. The social regeneration of communities drives

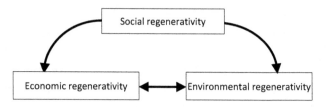

Figure 5.2 Social regenerativity as the engine of sustainability transitions.

the three pillars of the sustainability transition process (see Figure 5.2). Regenerating communities' social well-being results in all those social benefits that flow from greater neighborhood security, including education, gender issues, increased personal freedom, and political empowerment. This social regenerativity drives economic regeneration through improved security and freedoms, which allows economic activity to expand, and people to move and work more freely, and also offering alternatives to the destructive problem of young people being drawn into lives of violence, corruption, and organized criminality. Finally, social regenerativity drives the environmental regeneration that comes when people can move safely to tend to their neighborhood gardens and produce food locally. Figure 5.2 depicts these dynamics that flow from HM's focus on social regenerativity. The cascading benefits that accrue economically and environmentally would not occur without the circular social regenerativity that is enabled by the HM business model

Being a regenerative entrepreneur in this social context of 'three pillar circularity' means that personal stories, histories, and purposes can be drawn on to create multiple forms of benefits that restore the resilience of natural and social systems. Our two HM entrepreneurs possess a range of competencies that, while not unusual in isolation, together provide a rich source for innovative connection and relationship building. Circularity is frequently portrayed as a technical strategy for developing sustainability; in this example, however, we see the power of social circularity and the kinds of sustainability and ethical competencies for building the social infrastructure of a very innovative form of circular business model.

Regenerative purposes and self-stories

Innovation at HM is seen as a creative process of applying values to achieve the enterprise mission of building community through reduction in gun violence. The means for achieving that purpose, the HM business model, is to upcycle gun metal into beautiful consumer products. The simplicity and strength of this mission is so immediately appealing that it is easy to see why our entrepreneurs should feel so identified with that vision and why the alignment between personal and organizational values was so evident. What is less evident, but no less salient, is the role of self-story and personal history in the success of the HM enterprise. A complex web of personal motivations lies behind the commitment, energy, and imagination that both Simon and Jacqueline bring to their work. Their personal stories are diverse and, in most cases, radically different from the individual lives of the stakeholders that they work with. But there is a red thread of connection through their empathy, one might even say compassion, for others and the shared sense of humanity that those emotions engender.

The HM business model not only injects a regenerative social sustainability into the communities, it brings a regenerative and revitalizing balance to the entrepreneurs themselves. Working in the international development and sustainability fields can be a draining, if not exhausting vocation. While this is true of the HM enterprise, there is also a rejuvenating side to the work that restores faith in people and in the power of community resourcefulness. Regenerativity is not only about revitalizing the exterior worlds of ecologies, communities, and economies. It is also about regenerating the interior qualities that power personal inspiration and commitment. Jacqueline mentioned that there was a big emphasis on developing staff's "self-leadership" capacities. The IM aim is that staff define and develop "their own priorities and goals" and that these objectives become the orienting framework for their own performance and work goals. These interior goals become as, or even more, important than the formal organizational goals of KPIs. In speaking with the HM entrepreneurs, it was evident that the regenerative power of their work operated at all levels from the specific task objectives and program goals through to the business strategies and business models through to the guiding values and overall mission and purpose of the enterprise. Figure 5.3 draws attention to how entrepreneurs' personal backgrounds invigorated each of these work levels. The figure also speculates that the organization story and 'corporate image' of IM plays a similar role from the organizational and management side of the equation.

Figure 5.3 Personal self-story, organizational image, and regenerativity.

Emancipation, regenerativity, and entrepreneurship

Entrepreneurship has been likened to a form of emancipation that frees people from the constraints of the status quo. For example, Rindova, Barry, and Ketchen (2009) take the perspective that:

> Viewing entrepreneurial projects as emancipatory efforts focuses on understanding the factors that cause individuals to seek to disrupt the status quo and change their position in the social order in which they are embedded.
>
> (Rindova et al., 2009, p. 478)

The HM enterprise can be seen as disruptive not only in relation to the violent systems of corruption and criminality that characterize the suburbs and towns in which it operates. It is disruptive of the culture of weapons manufacturing, the geopolitical causes of community violence and the flow of drugs, illegal financial proceeds, and human trafficking that cut across international borders. The organizational ethic of HM disrupts assumptions that problems always lie elsewhere and that we are not intimately connected with each other. The global nature of the HM circularity model disrupts the view that economy sets the contexts and priorities for society. For example, extractive economies not only instrumentalize nature and ecological systems, that is, consider them as resources for making a profit, but they also instrumentalize 'human resources'. In Triple Bottom Line terminology, extractive economies, whenever it is legally possible, prioritize profits over people and planet. The social regeneration model of HM flips these priorities. It does not leave profit or financial responsibilities out of the picture; rather, it sets human communities as the beneficiary to be prioritized. The socially and ecologically extractive approach that underpins a sizable proportion of international trade is disrupted by HM's offer of socially regenerative forms of renewal. This injection of regenerativity extends stakeholders' sense of connection and responsibility towards other individuals and other communities, and towards future generations, irrespective of where they might be placed in the circular loop of regeneration.

Case questions

1. What are some of the strengths and weaknesses for a business, and alternatively for an individual staff member, in having a strong alignment between personal and organizational purposes?
2. In what ways is it useful to talk of economic *and* social *and* environmental regenerativity?
3. How does HM contribute to regenerative sustainability in each of these three areas?
4. What strategies used by Jacqueline and Simon do you find to be the most persuasive? Do you also sometimes use similar strategies in your work or studies?
5. The case of Jacqueline shows that self-story and self-image can be important for many distinct aspects of professional work. In what areas of her work do you see the influence of her own personal background experiences? Are there any ways that your own upbring and formative life experiences have impacted on your won major life decisions and choices?

Workshop exercises

Exercise 1   Timely Advice

There must be a better way to make the things we want, a way that doesn't spoil the sky, or the rain or the land.

– Paul McCartney

The challenge

Reflecting on our professional purpose is not something we do often enough, if at all. The contributions we make to our own personal history and to our community through our work are significant. But it is all too frequently possible to end up in a job, workplace, or even profession without having done much deliberation about core purpose beforehand. One way to think about the expression of core values is that they can have a pivotal impact during those times when important decisions need to be made. The expression or non-expression of values is critical, for example, when one needs to choose which job to apply for, which organization to join, or which group to commit to. Hence, reflecting on our purpose and then deliberately seeking out the work, the company, the career we want will help in being true to who we are, or want to be. The challenge is to reflect on our key purpose and see how we can make choices and do things that are aligned with that core purpose.

What does this exercise make possible?

This exercise helps you to reflect on your work and career purpose.

Time:

45 mins

Structure of Exercise:

Working individually and in pairs

1. **Opening invitation:**

    Invite the class to be creative about developing a sense of purpose in their work. Join in with the exercise and do not censure your thinking about what that purpose might be.

2. **Materials and spaces:**

    *   Can be done in class or online.
    *   Each participant needs to take notes – computer, or pen and paper.

3. **Group participation and configuration:**

    *   Working as individual and pairs.

4. **Sequence of steps and time allocation:**

    Step 1 Working individually, write a response to the following scenario (no self-censoring of your thoughts, no self-criticism). Imagine that you are now 30 years into your future. You feel that you have done everything that you could to explore your potential, contribute to family and community, and achieve your life purpose. You have worked hard and done everything you could to be successful 30 years in the future. Describe what this purpose is (its main aspects, goals, what you should do and not do, etc.). (10 mins)

Step 2 Imagine that your 30-year older self comes back and appears to you in a dream and gives you advice about achieving this purpose. Write down what they would say? (No self-censoring of your thoughts, no self-criticism.) (10 mins)

Step 3 Take the advice of your future self and create a list of values that you need to achieve that purpose. Give examples of how these values will guide your daily behavior. (10mins)

Step 4 Share in pairs and participate in class discussion.

5. **Tips and traps:**
   - Your purpose is about you but, of course, each of us is connected to others and to the world we live in, so our purpose can involve all of that. The trap is that we can assume our purpose does not involve others or other aspects of the environment we live in.

6. **Variations:**
   - Run the exercise for just 1 year into the future to make it more concrete and foreseeable.

7. **Suggested extension materials:**
   - Use the Ikigai Tribe framework to prompt participants (available at www.ikigaitribe.com)

Exercise 2   I Did it My Way

Life is not measured by the number of breaths you take but by the moments that take your breath away.

— Maya Angelou

The challenge

To reflect on your life journey and how it shapes the life choices you make.

What does this exercise make possible?

Reflecting on one's life journey is useful at any time. It is especially helpful to think about the experiences you have had through life and their impact when deciding on vocational and educational plans. This exercise makes possible a deeper sense of our strengths, abilities, and personal styles of doing things, appreciating, and enjoying life.

Time: 50 mins

1. **Opening invitation:**
    Invite participants to connect with their personal histories and reflect on how their self-story might influence their work decisions and contributions.

2. **Materials and spaces:**
    Use the Appendices in Mary Gentile's 2010 book *Giving Voice to Values* to develop a self-story.

3. **Group participation and configuration:**
    If you are willing, share it with someone who can support you to make your vision a reality.

4. **Sequence of Steps and Time Allocation:**

5. **Self-Knowledge, Self-Image, and Alignment**
    Instructions to the exercise participants.

    Step 1: Generate a "self-story" or personal narrative using the prompts set out in Table 5.1 (15mins):

    Step 2: Share your story in groups of three. (3 × 3 mins = 10 mins)

Table 5.1 Prompts for generating a "self-story"

Childhood	Life Choices	Occupational Experiences
What were your family and parental influences?	What were some of the first decisions you remember making?	What were your first work experiences?
Where did you grow up?	Why did you make your educational choices?	What was the attitude towards work in your family?
What was your cultural and community environment?	What peer group(s) did you spend time together with as an adolescent?	What are you good at in work?
How stable was your upbringing?	What hobbies or interests have you enjoyed and/or developed?	What people have influenced your educational/work choices?
Who were your role models?	What were the earliest thoughts you had about your life purpose?	How do you like to occupy your time outside of work?
What was the impact of your schooling?	What challenges have you overcome in your life?	What do you want to achieve personally through your work?

Step 3: Discuss in your group how your self-story motivates you to work towards your educational professional goals. (3 × 3 = 10 mins)

Step 4: As a class discuss how we can utilize the strengths, preferences, and personal qualities we possess to voice our values in ways that suit who we are, that build on our self-story. (15 mins)

6. **Tips and Traps:**
   - There is no need to get into the details of deeply personal events or issues here. Give some cautionary introduction that participants should not share information that is deeply personal or that they would later regret sharing. Also discuss the need for consideration of confidentiality and that what is shared should not leave the educational setting.

7. **Variations:**
   - Run the exercise as a personal journal assignment that is developed through a course.
   - The exercise can be done online or onsite.

8. **Suggested extension materials:**
   - Set reading from the Gentile book *Giving Voice to Values* and videos specifically concerned with self-story.
   - https://ethicsunwrapped.utexas.edu/video/pillar-5-self-knowledge-and-alignment

---

Notes

1 We use *social-ecological value network* as a more accurate term for the web of human and ecological relationships in which all companies are immersed. The usual jargon of "supply chain" simply does not capture the profound interpenetration of biophysical systems that underpins all elements of economic production and consumption. The systems that HM is working with are not just about mechanical chains of supply and demand pressures. The human and the ecological are intimately interconnected in multilayered networks, not linear chains. The environmental, communal, and ethical factors involved in their work are complex and inclusive of all kinds of emotional, ecological, intellectual, physical value that cannot be reduced to the economic forces of linear supply and demand models.

2 Based on the story of Wendy https://humanium-metal.com/16-days-of-activism/wendy-the-story-of-a-survivor/

References

Humanium Metal. (2020). *The Striker. IM Swedish Development Partner* [Online]. Retrieved from https://humanium-metal.com/our-impact/

Rindova, V., Barry, D., & Ketchen, J. D. J. (2009). Entrepreneuring as emancipation. *Academy of Management Review, 34*(3), 477–491. Retrieved from http://search.ebscohost.com/login.aspx?direct=true&db=buh&AN=40632647&site=ehost-live

Sternad, D., Kennelly, J. J., & Bradley, F. (2016). *Digging Deeper: How Purpose-Driven Enterprises Create Real Value*. Austin, TX: Greenleaf.

6

THE NATURAL WEALTH OF SEAWEED

This chapter explores how regenerative entrepreneurs effectively enact their personal and organizational values in daily practices and conversations. We tell the story of two entrepreneurs who escaped from the contemporary business world, reflected on their personal motivations and business goals, and built a regenerative organization – The Seaweed Company. Our entrepreneurs navigated many ethical challenges to grasp hold of the immense opportunities that regenerative sustainability opens. We look at how our protagonists provide enabling arguments to counter inhibiting reasons (GVV's 'rationalizations') that stymie the expression of core values. Our analysis of the case considers how different perspectives interact and contest with each other to build persuasive conversations that challenge prevailing unsustainable practices.

DOI: 10.4324/9781003330660-6

THE CASE OF THE SEAWEED COMPANY IN BRIEF

Organization name: The Seaweed Company (TSC)
Year of founding: 2018
Website: https://www.theseaweedcompany.com/
Type of organization: For-profit, steward ownership foundation
Purpose/mission of organization: TSC's mission is to contribute to a sustainable world through working with the most common of all plants – seaweed. All impacts – economic, social and environmental are positively beneficial for all human and natural stakeholders
Industry sector: Biotechnology, aquaculture, agriculture, health supplements and skincare products, with a focus on the food industry and food value network
Services: A vertically integrated biotech company operating with the seaweed supply chain, with the development of value products in the fields of aquaculture, health supplements and skincare products
Locations: TSC has farms and operations in The Netherlands, Ireland, Morocco, India and Greenland.
Impact and achievements: TSC is an impact company that prioritizes environmental and social impact above financial goals. TSC farms sequester 450 tonnes of CO_2 per year. Winner of the 2023 Sustainable Food Awards in the category Sustainable Food Ingredient – SeaMeat®, a seaweed ingredient that supplements and replaces 20–30% of meat in meat products.

The power of ethical conversations

This chapter explores how regenerative entrepreneurs effectively enact their personal and organizational values in daily practices and conversations. We tell the story of two entrepreneurs who "escaped" from the contemporary business world, reflected on their personal motivations and business goals, and built a regenerative organization –The Seaweed Company (TSC). Ethical conversations have played a crucial role in establishing, developing, and maintaining this innovative company. Ethical conversations are interactive communications that explicitly discuss values and the importance of values for achieving core personal and corporate purposes. In looking at the role of conversations in building regenerative businesses, we will focus on arguments that enable and inhibit the expression of values.

The Seaweed Company

The Seaweed Company is a privately-owned steward-ownership company that operates in the food industry network. Founded in 2018, TSC's mission is to contribute to a sustainable world through working with the most common of all plants – seaweed. Seaweed is a macroalgae rich in minerals, vitamins and polysaccharides, sometimes also amino acids, proteins, peptides, polyphenols, and fatty acids. This makes it an incredibly rich natural resource with strong health properties and a valuable material for many different applications, such as the production of food, fuel, cosmetics, and pharmaceuticals. Additionally, seaweed has immense potential to support the regeneration of marine environments. Being regenerative in nature, seaweed provides a more sustainable alternative to many existing product ingredients and materials. Seaweed has the potential to contribute positively to the stabilization of six of the nine planetary boundaries (PBs) (Flannery, 2017; Yong, Thien, Rupert, & Rodrigues, 2022). With around 12,000 species (40 commercially grown) growing in various kinds of waters, such as oceans, brackish and freshwater environments, it is a flexible crop that does not need land nor additional freshwater to grow (hence resulting in a positive impact on the PBs of 'land system change' and 'freshwater use'). Since the Earth is 70% covered by seawater, this is a huge benefit. As it grows, it uses photosynthesis to turn CO_2 into biomass, reducing the amount of carbon in the atmosphere and the ocean (positive impact on PBs 'climate change' and 'ocean acidification'). Since seaweed does not need pesticides or fertilizers to grow, and since it absorbs nutrients such as nitrogen and phosphorus from the water, it also helps mitigating ocean eutrophication (positive impact on PB 'biogeochemical flows'). Seaweed also play a key role in the provision of ecosystem services as it forms an integral part of a complex food web and offers habitat, nursery grounds and shelter for many marine species, leading to greater biodiversity (positive impact on PB 'biosphere integrity').

Regenerative solutions

Through a mix of biological and technological expertise and facilities in countries such as Ireland, Morocco, India, and the Netherlands, TSC has learned how to effectively produce, collect, and process seaweed on a commercial scale. The company mostly builds business-to-business (B2B) commercial relationships on an international scale and works with local farmers, food producers, and consumer goods and food retailers. They focus on three operations: growing and harvesting seaweed; creating seaweed-based products; and collaboratively delivering value and impact through their seaweed solutions to partners. The company does this by co-innovating with its commercial partners to develop regenerative solutions that sequestrate GHG emissions and generates positive social-ecological benefits for local communities. Some examples of solutions they produce, and sell, are bio-stimulants, healthy food ingredients for both humans and animals, carbon removal credits, and farming solutions for transitioning to regenerative agriculture.

The company is vertically integrated through the whole value chain from the point of local production and cultivation of seaweed seedlings to harvesting, processing, product manufacturing, and retailing. For example, after the seaweed has been cultivated in one of their farms in India, Morocco, Ireland, or The Netherlands, it is harvested and removed from its growing substrates, either by hand or with the help of a harvesting machine. After harvest, the seaweed is dried and weighed, with only 17% of the original mass being left after drying. The dried seaweed is then turned into products sold to customers around the world. These products have a positive environmental and social impact. For example, one line of products supports farmers to accelerate the transition toward regenerative agriculture. There are many innovations at various points in the supply chain to optimize positive benefits to various stakeholders. For example, seaweed certificates are publicly issued so that individuals can adopt an amount of seaweed that has been harvested and dried. These certificates then support the company's mission and accelerate their work and impact. Another example of innovation is that, at all stages in the production process, products and materials are auditable, traceable, and verifiable to ensure quality, fault diagnoses, and customer communication.

A collaborative business model

By focusing on both profit and social-ecological purpose, TSC develops itself as a business and contributes to the sustainability of the communities in which it operates and sells. Its products capture carbon, regenerate marine ecosystems, develop local seaside communities, and generate sustainable revenues and healthy profit margins. The company directly employs over 30 people across the globe, but its impact is amplified through its B2B and local community partnerships. As a for-profit business, the company competes in the global marketplace, but also focuses on what might be called its collaborative advantage (Kanter, 1994). First, the company's leadership aims for long-term relationships with their customers based on joint business plans to co-create common goals and plans for growing businesses together. Second, the company does not primarily sell organic products but sustainability solutions, creative concepts, and innovative expertise. They help their partners to create not only monetary value but also ecological and social value. Finally, every project the company launches must be "environmentally restorative, socially just and economically inclusive". Hence, all their operations must be vetted on these three sustainability pillars. If a project looks financially promising but does not reach regenerative environmental and equable social criteria, it does not proceed.

The entrepreneurs

Joost Wouters – Founder and 'SeaEO'

Following his desire to be an entrepreneur, Joost left his position as director of a multinational company around 25 years ago. He decided to follow his passion and create a truly sustainable business. After travelling the world gaining insight into sustainability ventures, he started his own consultancy firm where he focused on sustainability transitioning in small and medium-sized enterprises (SMEs). However, a sense of frustration set in quickly when Joost realized that, while good advice was being given to business leaders, little was being acted on and implemented to the degree it could have been. He felt he needed to take matters into his own hands. Driven by a sense of integrity and accountability for his time here on Earth, he began researching starting a business that would have a positive impact on society, environment, and economy. In 2018, he founded TSC together with his friends and colleagues Edwin Sneekes and Stefan Kraan. The journey of starting and developing the company has, however, been anything but straightforward.

Joost had extensive experience of working in the conventional business world and, even though people around him were supportive, starting such an ambitious and ground-breaking business necessarily involves enormous obstacles. Joost and his co-founders realized that they were pioneers, and that there was no blueprint nor established route to follow. This highlighted the need for technological, biological, and financial innovation. Leaving his old career path behind, he dedicated himself to understanding and analyzing the new market. During this time, he had no income, but he received unqualified support from his family and pressed on with founding the company. With high hopes, strong motivation, and a deep recognition that it was the right thing to do, Joost moved forward.

Wouter Zwagemakers – Head of Commerce

Wouter has been working at TSC since September 2020. He has a broad professional background working in businesses from industrial engineering to finance and strategy. Before joining TSC, he worked for 15 years for large corporations, where he was often involved in strategy, business development, and finance roles. For example, he worked as head of strategy at a large Dutch multinational. While enjoying the work of improving corporate responsibility and supporting the change process, Wouter felt the urge to contribute to building innovative nature-based solutions for the global challenges that we face. To a certain extent, Wouter also felt a misalignment of values and vision between his own sense of success and what he saw as the typical understanding of success at the enterprise level.

Having spent quite some time to fine-tune his personal purpose around the Nature–Food–Technology nexus, Wouter actively started engaging with business initiatives that were working for nature- and technology-based sustainability solutions. During this search he came across TSC, a company that shared his values, ambitions, and principles. He contacted Joost and before he could think too much about the consequences, he found himself volunteering to assist Joost and his co-founders in building up the company. Wouter felt intuitively drawn to building a new business and he wanted to be a key player in that new story. On the other hand, changing career was easier said than done. Like most other people, he enjoys financial wealth and the security it brings. Risking all of that for a new and uncertain career was challenging, especially when he had a family to provide for. As Wouter puts it, making such a decision "It really feels in the stomach". But Wouter is neither crazy nor an idealist. He is pragmatic. While working on a voluntary basis for TSC, he successively started letting go of his old business connections. During the transition period, Wouter ensured an income from his previous work through a sabbatical period where he was still partly paid. This pragmatism helped him overcome the financial risks and uncertainty about where the new career path would take him. However, he was driven by a strong sense of purpose, and he sat down and wrote a letter to his children explaining his decision, committing to working for a more sustainable world and to doing what he could to safeguard their future. He keeps this letter and occasionally reads it to himself to motivate and remind himself of his core purpose in working for sustainable and regenerative solutions. For him, TSC is a means to that end.

Wouter played a significant role in the early development of the company. He began recording all the ideas, plans, and visions that were, to that point, in the heads of the founders. He distilled these ideas into a brief paper summarizing the founding organizational principles and values. It was this document that would shape the company's emerging business model. In March 2021, his volunteer engagements changed into full-time employment. This was a huge move that involved a lot of career risk, but he was now captured by the vision and passion for pursuing his core values of responsibility, sustainability, and vision. He took up tasks such as seeking investments, structuring the company's finances, building the corporate brand and its vision, communicating that vision, the company's story, and the potential of its products and services.

Critical systems thinkers

Both Joost and Wouter call themselves systems thinkers who question the status quo, asking if what we are doing will bring us closer to our core goals of social development, well-being, environmental sustainability, and community peace and justice. They engage critically with the questions of business and working life purpose. Is it, they ask, normal and desirable that the success of a business, or a society, is driven by a single measure of macro-economic growth, the famous index of national financial transactions called Gross Domestic Product (GDP)? Is a capitalist economic system single-mindedly focused on growth and profit truly efficient? Is it valid that big corporations prioritize their financial success over the impacts they have on human communities and ecological systems? Without challenging these assumptions, the economic system and commercial businesses will continue to marginalize sustainability goals and the pursuit of intergenerational prosperity and resilient natural environments.

If we consider Wouter, for example, it is clear that his capacity for critical questioning grew out of his adolescent and young adulthood experiences. For as long as he can remember, he has been curious, open-minded, and wanting to understand why and how things are connected. In his early 20s, when he was a student, he wanted to contribute to the drive toward sustainability and find out why and how events in one part of the world lead to cascading change in very distant parts. Both Joost and Wouter are deeply aware of the scientific findings on how the globalized economic systems, natural ecologies, and societies across the world are connected. Through their business and close affiliation with its stakeholders they have both experienced the interdependencies between financial, societal, and environmental well-being. This personal experience motivates both Joost and Wouter to build the values and guiding principles that recognize these connections into TSC's business model.

The Seaweed Company: Its impact & values

TSC's founding created a unique opportunity. Starting from scratch, the founders had the chance to design a company "fit for the 22nd century", a company that is long-term-oriented, that cares about future generations, that knows about the limits of the Earth, and that aims to thrive over intergenerational timeframes. Being a company focused on creating meaningful impact, they have, next to financial objectives, used the triple-layered business model canvas (economic, social, and environmental) and built into the company's business model a set of social and ecological impact goals that should be met by 2030. These goals are:

- 25 million tons of CO_2e mitigated
- 4,000 seaweed farming jobs
- 500,000 "blue farmers"[1]
- 1 million hectares of land regenerated
- 25 million animals improved health & well-being annually
- 3,500 hectares of seaweed farms globally

They have also created means for measuring impacts through different metrics:

(1) CO_2e mitigation: Since they know that every ton of seaweed absorbs 120 kg of CO_2, 2 kg of nitrogen, and 0.2 kg of phosphorus, they can calculate the amount of CO_2e sequestrated from their harvests.
(2) Community development: By working directly with coastal communities, they employ local families in the seaweed value chain. In this way they can see how many families have been supported and how many people are involved in their operations.
(3) Ocean regeneration: Seaweed reduces ocean acidification and promotes marine biodiversity by regenerating the ocean floor. Therefore, they can measure the number of hectares of ocean that have been regenerated through their seaweed plantations.

TSC's impact approach is built on the IRIS+ principles developed by the Global Impact Investing Network's (GIIN) and they expect to publish their first impact report in 2023. IRIS+ is an impact investment system that manages and measures organizational operations for optimal sustainability impact. IRIS+ considers governance policy, stakeholder engagement, stakeholder interests, transparency, additive value, and financial accounts.

Along with tangible performance metrics, intangible key values indicators were benchmarked from other values-driven businesses, such as *Patagonia* and *Tony's Chocolonely*. The set of principles that Joost, Wouter, and the rest of the team formalized in the building phase of the company underpins all the core strategies and operations of the organization. They are shared by everyone in the organization and guide employees on how to act when they are faced with decision-making points that might jeopardize the core purpose or main strategic direction of the business. The principles are:

• We are hooked on seaweed
• We combine passion & expertise to create seaweed solutions with meaningful impact
• Everything we do is economically inclusive, socially just and environmentally restorative
• We work with nature
• We realize we need speed and scale to have impact

- We put value on a sustainable, traceable, and reliable supply chain of seaweed
- We are open, transparent, and inclusive
- We see everyone involved as ambassadors of The Seaweed Company
- We are building a company for the 22nd century
- We take our role as pioneers seriously and love to spread our passion for seaweed

From these principles a set of core values can be identified, namely: (1) Respect: respecting nature and people, (2) Honesty: promoting honesty and transparency, (3) Creativity: fostering creativity and innovation, (4) Integrity: having integrity across multiple situations, and (5) Responsibility: extending the circle of responsibility. These values are regarded as non-negotiable, and it is important that internal and external stakeholders consciously adopt and align with them. One way to build this values-alignment capacity quickly is by recruiting and hiring people that already hold these values and commitments. Both Joost and Wouter hold the view that such strategies have enabled the company to create a powerful corporate culture and a values base that is strongly aligned with their vision.

Steward ownership

An essential dimension of the long-term commitment that Joost and Wouter have toward the company is the organization's ownership structure. One-fifth of the company is owned by a stewardship foundation that has employees as members. This kind of ownership, called *steward ownership*, ensures that the company cannot be sold or bought out. The foundation ensures that short-term commitments and financial goals do not supplant the reason the organization was founded. It also places ownership responsibilities in the hands of stewards or members, for example, employees, customers, investors, who are key stakeholders of the company. Voting rights cannot be sold and profit serves purpose because they cannot be privatized and are reinvested in the company or donated to serve the mission of the company. Investors and founders are fairly compensated; however, they cannot sell their shares in the company and so financial incentives serve to support mission and purpose in benefiting communities and the ecological systems that provide for them.

Steward-ownership are legally committed to two key principles (Raisher, 2022): i) *Self-governance* – Steward-owned businesses are controlled by people who are actively engaged in or strictly connected to the company's mission (the "stewards"). The company's control can only be held by stewards because they must always own most voting rights. ii) *Profits serve purpose*: Profits are a means to an end – how their purpose can be furthered – and not an end in and of themselves. A steward-owned company "belongs to itself and its purpose" (Bonan et al., 2020, p. 6), allowing it to be stewarded toward what is best for the company and the society it is embedded in.

The form of ownership adopted when setting up an organization is the most important single factor that influences the long-term sustainability status of that business. Ownership matters deeply in terms of whether or not an organization's purpose prioritizes social-ecological benefits. For-profits businesses, especially those that have limited liability legal status, typically focus on the profit motive and place social and environmental objectives further down the list of corporate priorities. Alternative ownership structures, such as cooperatives, B-corps and for-Benefit Corporations, foundations and steward-ownership models, are set up to meet a much broader set of priorities. By founding TSC on a steward-ownership basis, Joost and Wouter are putting their core values into the legal identity of the organization and that single act declares loudly who they are and what they are committed to.

Analysis – Rationalizations and sustainability

Every reason to accept the offer

TSC's principles and values both inspire, and are inspired by, its leaders and employees to pursue their regenerative work. However, that does not mean opposing social entities, structures, and obstacles can be easily avoided. One area where values can be especially important for informing the quality of decision-making is in investment and financing. This is also an area where rationalizations are frequently encountered.

In Chapter 2 we looked at the kinds of rhetorical arguments, justifications, and rationalizations designed to disengage us from the outcomes of our poor decision-making and lack of ethical commitment to our core values and purposes. Rationalizations are reasons that argue for inaction, disengagement, and moral distancing. They are arguments, usually quite sensible and defensible in themselves, that silence or at least weaken the expression of core values. Rationalizations act to disengage us from the moral implications of our choices and actions, they function to justify past acts, to neutralize us from empathetic feelings and critical judgments. In their strongest form rationalizations are arguments offered to "explain an act of wrongdoing as morally justifiable" (Schnatterly, Gangloff, & Tuschke, 2018, p. 2049). But "wrongdoing", especially when associated with legality, is an extremely low bar to set when considering issues of values and ethical commitments. When higher standards are involved, rationalizations can act to undermine core moral principles and aspirations that go way beyond basic legal codes.

In the context of sustainability, the actions that businesses need to undertake are not often legally regulated (although this is changing) but depend on the voluntary adoption of sustainability-orientated strategies and innovations. Rationalizations can act to weaken these voluntary commitments and corrupt the vision and mission that drives sustainability performance. The act of voicing values often involves having to overcome these silencing arguments. In the following sections, we detail two instances where the persuasive power of inhibiting rationalizations needed to be countered. One case occurred at the business level of investment relationships and the other at the personal level of personal 'voice'.

Early on during the investment-raising process, some venture capitalists saw TSC's financial potential. Joost and his founding partners talked with the investor for months and both parties got to know each other very well. However, when they finally saw the initial offer, they realized that things were not as they expected. The terms of agreement were not at all what TSC either needed nor wanted. They were based on conditions that would be harmful to the company and to Joost's founding vision. The terms were driven by financial returns and were built on a short-term perspective where the economic aspects would be prioritized over both the social and environmental aspects, and where the investors would get a big share of the company when it became profitable. The capital to be invested was a large amount, but the terms did not align with TSC's ownership model or mission. Joost and the other founders could have used that capital to place the start-up on a very secure financial footing. The investors wanted to support the company's development, but it was all about the financial opportunity.

Joost wanted his new venture to succeed, but having major investors who were not aligned with the core values and mission of the business could dilute its ethical commitments and mission.

In responding to this dilemma there are many rationalizations that Joost, his co-founders, and trusted allies could put to themselves and to each other that argued for accepting the conventional, profit-driven investment partner. Such rationalizations can take many forms but typically they fall into a small number of categories. Before finishing our story about the venture capital investors let us look at some examples of these rationalization categories and give some illustrative examples of what Joost and his team members might have said to argue their way into accepting the offer.

1. *Standard practice*: "There is nothing wrong here. This is a typical investment offer that is a conventional and legally sound way of raising money. All venture capital comes from sources like this and if I do not accept this, someone else will."
2. *Materiality*: "There will be no negative impact of accepting this money if we keep our vision and principles together. No one gets hurt."
3. *Locus of responsibility*: "I am the one responsible for making sure this venture succeeds so I should accept this funding. It's my responsibility to ensure the security of the start-up because so many other are taking a risk in working for me."
4. *Locus of loyalty*: "My first responsibility is to be loyal to my company and my people. There are so many who depend on the success of this venture. That obligation of loyalty comes before my preferences about the alignment or misalignment of investment values."
5. *Legality*: "It's entirely legal so there is no problem with accepting the offer. We will just use this conventional money to start with and then drop this investor once we get started."
6. *Compartmentalization*: "We can and should separate the values that guide our financial and investment activities from those that govern long-term sustainability and operational goals."
7. *Risk*: "This whole venture is risky. I need to make our financial foundation as secure as possible and if that means accepting money from disagreeable sources then so be it."
8. *Denial of harm*: "I am a value-based leader and I have the skills to make sure no one and no ecosystem is harmed if I accept this funding."

When new ventures are created, the initial conditions of the start-up activities can be vulnerable to such arguments. As time goes by, the power of financial relationships and the voice of key investors and financial stakeholders often grows in importance and the "process bias" of incremental change can lead an organization step-by-step away from the founding vision. The influence of these pressures can result in a dilution of aspirations and principled intents. In the case of TSC this has not occurred.

And what did the founders decide?

The moment the team saw the terms of agreement they could barely believe their eyes. It was not what they had been discussing through all these weeks of negotiations. They asked themselves if this was really happening. Would the future of the company be put in jeopardy if they refused this offer? They started discussing the ethical dilemma internally to reaffirm their own commitments and find allies in dealing with the dilemma. They then arranged a virtual meeting with the investors to clarify what the offer meant and the basis on which it was made. Their worst expectations were confirmed. When Joost said there was a basic misunderstanding in that the terms of the offer were not aligned with the mission and values of the company, the response of the investor was to rationalize and defend their viewpoint. The investors argued that this is how things were done in the venture capital investment world. The terms of the agreement were financially advantageous for both parties and compliant with all legal regulations and industry standards. Joost, Wouter, and the other founders made their point very clear and said, "We are a purpose driven company and do not want to be subject to a financial force, nor do we want to be steered by capitalism". The implications of rejecting the offer were significant for a start-up business and so the meeting ended with a resolution that all parties would reflect on the way forward.

After the meeting, someone from TSC called a representative from the investment company to tell them separately one-on-one that the deal was not going to happen. Joost and his co-founders have rejected approximately €3,500,000€ from mainstream investors because of the non-alignment in values and the differing sense of purpose. However, one important aspect of this seminal event was that Joost and several of the company's founders subsequently maintained their relationship with the investor and would at some point meet to reflect upon the whole situation over a coffee. The expression of voice and the power of rationalizations are managed pragmatically to reinforce core values while also not burning any bridges with investment markets. The affirmation of values and the reinforcement of TSC's ethical voice increases self-efficacy and individuals' capacity to voice their values in the future.

Figure 6.1 sets out this dilemma in terms of the rationalizing versus enabling arguments and other support factors based on TSC's culture. The figure shows the process by which the ethical dilemma of whether or not to accept the investment offer was taken. The initial challenge to core values initiates a series of conversations and dialogues where rationalizations and enabling arguments are exchanged. The conversations result in the strengthening of core values and the decision to reject the investment funds. Finally, following up actions are taken to ensure that the relationship between the parties is retained.

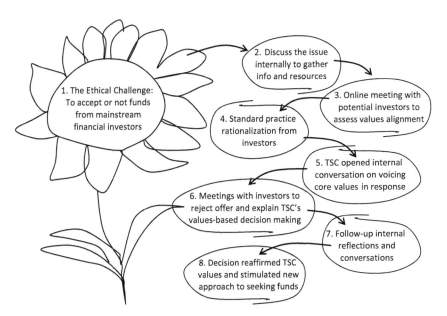

Figure 6.1 The mainstream investment case: Countering the rationalization process and strengthening TSC's capacity to voice its core values.

The outcome of the decision to reject the initial investment offer was a particularly useful one for the company in that it reaffirmed their core values and made it clear that they needed to innovate and seek investments in a different way. This decision meant they had to be far more creative in raising investment funds. They shifted their investment strategy and began to concentrate on getting the story of the company across and communicating their mission to investors who shared their values. Wouter also came up with the notion of crowdfunding through a kind of values-based donation that he called "seaweed carbon certificates". Donators who buy a certificate get to see that their donations result in a regenerative impact by absorbing carbon dioxide and increasing marine biodiversity.

Hearing the voice of an intern

Since this incident, TSC has given even more priority to the public communication of values in recruitment, partnership collaboration, and stakeholder engagement. It is also why they actively help their employees once they are on board with how to use these values as guidance in ethical dilemmas. During the onboarding phase, where new employees are inducted into the culture of the organization, and during the first years in the company, the founders frequently communicate and offer opportunities for discussing the company's core values. The purpose is to actively build a culture where employees feel confident that they can speak up when something concerns them or express novel ideas and not be afraid of being ostracized or blamed for a failure. This culture of psychological safety supports the building of an ethical and innovative culture. Feeling confident that you will be heard functions to promote the expression of normative values as well as creative ideas and innovations. This cuts across all levels of the organization, from Joost himself to the newest intern.

One incident that exemplifies this embedding of psychological safety in the culture of the company involved a young intern. The management team was presented with the idea of selling seaweed certificates for carbon offset at a general meeting of all company staff. A young intern was present at the meeting but did not say anything. After the meeting, however, the intern wrote a letter to Joost saying that the idea was not as well thought out as it might be and could easily be framed as a greenwashing exercise. Growing seaweed absorbs CO_2 but as soon as it's harvested it will begin to emit some of that CO_2 which ends up once again in the atmosphere. The problem was that the certificates gave the impression that the carbon was being sequestered and locked away for years. Joost immediately saw that the intern was completely right, and the next day they changed the concept. The intern was contacted and thanked for raising the issue. Today, Joost feels that one of his biggest roles is to make sure that they keep this culture of honesty and openness alive and to create a corporate culture that encourages personal autonomy and the free exchange of ideas and values. There are many spinoffs from developing this kind of corporate culture. Joost finds that employees develop a sense of autonomy and self-efficacy whatever their work role might be. With autonomy, employees can make their own choices and act to solve dilemmas that frequently arise in one form or another.

Rationalizations and business-as-usual

Acting ethically is not simple, not even for purpose-driven businesses. Regenerative businesses constantly work to build new markets that offer real value, that is, social-ecological and economic value, to customers and stakeholders. The movement away from extractive economies advances through the creation of new commercial environments that prioritize social-ecological over financial benefits. This shift obviously creates dilemmas and conflicts because a radical reprioritization of benefits challenges the Business-As-Usual (BAU) profit motive demanded by conventional market values. Even in companies that pursue sustainability strategies of some kind, they typically prioritize and express these values through an economic lens. It is the business case for sustainability that still dominates, rather than the social or environmental case. It is the economic bottom line that still informs the default definition of business success. TSC is facing these dilemmas as well, but it navigates its way through these complexities by firmly holding to the north star of regenerativity. It is also important to note that making profits is on no account left out of the picture. In fact, the place of profits in decision-making is prioritized like any other business, but it is important only as a means for achieving benefits for social and ecological stakeholders. As a result, economic arguments and priorities do not act as rationalizations for downplaying other social and environmental values or goals. Communicating this to other stakeholders supports a shared understanding of the basis on which important TSC decisions and strategies

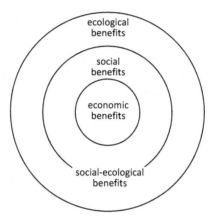

Figure 6.2 An embedded view on business sustainability.

will be made. Maximizing investors' ROI (return on investment) is not the purpose of TSC, but then its investors do not want it to be. They too, share in the embedded prioritization of the economic perspective within the social and ecological ones (see Figure 6.2). As more research evaluations are performed on the outcomes of sustainability transitions it becomes clear that long-term financial benefits are optimized through exactly this formula of prioritizing the social and ecological case. Ensuring that social-ecological returns are strategically highlighted makes it more likely that financial returns will be realized over the long term.

Ongoing conversations on these kinds of topics are frequently held around TSC. This is the single most important thing they can do to promote ethical enactment, to keep the conversation about values and principles alive. A prerequisite for this to happen is that the organizational environment is open enough for people to feel confident about expressing their opinions and engaging in values-based conversations.

Insights

This chapter has focused on the Giving Voice to Values (GVV) pillar of Reasons and Rationalizations for exploring the case of The Seaweed Company. TSC entrepreneurs have been guided by their core values in developing a regenerative business that goes beyond standard corporate purposes. The case shows how it is possible to pursue regenerative goals and remain true to core sustainability values while finding competitive and collaborative advantages in mainstream markets.

The interconnected nature of GVV pillars

The story of the founding and development of TSC illustrates the power of ethical commitments and the relevance of all the GVV pillars for the company and how Joost and Wouter have established its operations. The case also shows how interconnected the GVV pillars are. We have seen here how countering *rationalizations* with enabling arguments and firm reasons can lead to *values-based* conversations that open new possibilities or reaffirm existing commitments. Holding such conversations is a *choice* that helps to exercise one's own sense of *voice* and *self-efficacy* and, over time, this can lead to a broader awareness and greater skill in expressing core values as a *normal* function of everyday work. Our two entrepreneurs exemplify how working with their *personal strengths* played a huge role in the development of their regenerative vision. They possess both a strong critical capacity for not only questioning the BAU world but also a powerful visionary side that generates meaningful *purpose*. Together, these GVV pillars form a cultural recipe for building an ethical and regenerative organization.

Rationalization as enabling opportunity

The TSC case shows that motivating factors, such as a clear and strong purpose, can in themselves act as reasons for voicing your values. For instance, when evaluating the risk of leaving a fixed salary and a secure job against the benefits of building a regenerative business, it is hard not to fall into the pattern of rationalizing the safe route of continuing with BAU. It takes a lot of dedication and an innate knowledge of the 'right thing to do' to keep moving forward. On both a personal and a professional level, Joost and Wouter are driven by the purpose of contributing to the creation of a better, more sustainable world, and to safeguard it for their children and generations to come. Having this alignment between their personal and professional purposes from the start created reasons for emancipating themselves from the contemporary business world and gave them the tools and enabling arguments needed to face the risks and inhibiting rationalizations involved with making that decision.

Values-based decision-making during start-up

The start-up phase of a new venture is obviously crucial to its formative development as even the smallest event in the initial stages can have a huge influence on what the business will look like in its mature stages. In the same way, the TSC case highlights the importance of building the right culture and staying true to your values in the initial phase and early development of the business. The case shows that it is not enough to start working on your culture and values when your business has been developed, but that you will have to do so right from the start. This is especially true for regenerative businesses. The temptation of leaving the regenerative path and following the BAU path is greatest during the start-up phase, as enterprises are less resilient and more sensitive to forces that push the business into conventional way of doing things. By doing things right from the start, by writing down and practicing their organizational values at an early stage, Joost and Wouter set the company off on a regenerative path and made it possible to stay on this path, even when encountering strong headwinds. Their shared professional and organizational purpose, together with their strong organizational values, guide their decision-making today. These qualities have helped them build a strong corporate culture highly resistant to barrier shifting into more conventional business practices and consequently developing TSC into a successful regenerative business.

False dichotomies and regenerative entrepreneurship

The BAU perspective assumes that profit is prioritized over contending business purposes and that management must focus on optimizing the financial returns for investors. The existence of companies such as TSC shows that it is possible to elevate social and ecological goals while still ensuring financial success. Assuming that social-ecological responsibilities are in opposition to pecuniary interests is a false dichotomy because there is no inherent contradiction between the two. BAU market environments exert pressure on entrepreneurs to assume that financial returns must be pursued above all other priorities. Consequently, even when they hold sustainability and CSR-related values, BAU businesses, economists, and entrepreneurs can rationalize the neglect of social-ecological goals by claiming that economic growth and profit must come before everything else (Lipshaw, 2020; Thomas, 2023).

This process of false dichotomization, which has rationalized poor corporate governance, unethical business decisions, and unsustainable business operations for decades, is something that our entrepreneurs are aware of and are determined to avoid. They realize that, given the application of the right corporate strategies, setting ambitious social-ecological goals in business, and prioritizing those goals above financial ones can build financial sustainability rather than undercut it.

Proactively overcoming rationalizations

Walking the regenerative path in business requires ongoing commitment. Doing business as a way of working with your core values, for example, by using them to inform actions, decision, and conversations on a daily basis, strengthens the skills required to overcome rationalizations in the future. Joost and Wouter take the attitude that this ongoing opportunity for becoming aware of and enacting one's values is a source of joy and satisfaction in their business life. TSC has faced ethical problems in the past and they will do so in the future. They will face complex situations that challenge their organizational values and require the constant appraisal of how they balance environmental, social, and economic priorities. This balancing process is a core aspect of building and maintaining a regenerative business. TSC's impact statement clearly states their prioritization of their impact: "Everything we do is environmentally restorative, socially just and economically inclusive" (The Seaweed Company, 2023).

Clearly articulating its core priorities helps TSC to innovate solutions for overcoming rationalizations that might otherwise weaken corporate values. For example, since the very early days of its initial founding, TSC communications with both internal and external stakeholders have been characterized by an understanding that the prioritization of values is non-negotiable. As Joost puts it:

> From our early founding days through to today, we have kept our mission in mind in every decision made. This means that everything we do is measured by our positive ecological, social, and financial impact. We always have and continue to work with local communities and with nature, all the while operating in a financially viable manner to ensure the company's long-term, sustainable success.
>
> (The Seaweed Company, 2022)

Aligning regenerativity values with recruitment

While it is not unusual for a business to adopt values-based criteria in its recruitment practices, it is notable that TSC includes regenerativity in those values. By doing so, TSC is building a culture that supports stakeholder integrity and greater confidence to speak up when faced with ethical challenges. By learning about the organizational values early and practicing how to use them, TSC has developed a strong organizational culture that enables employees to voice their concerns in the face of rationalizations with confidence. This also leads to the social alignment of values not only between individual stakeholders and the organization and its various decision-making bodies but also in the temporal alignment of values over time (see Figure 2.2). For this to work well, TSC also created an organizational structure which empowers its employees and partners to feel included; accountable to each other but also entitled to raise their voice on any matter they want to. This alignment not only supports the inherent reproduction of TSC's internal culture, but also leads to an increased need and opportunity for connecting with external stakeholders. For instance, it becomes easier to attract values-aligned stakeholders, such as investors, community partners or employees, who share the same values and prioritizations.

Regenerativity through conversation

Overcoming rationalizations takes skill and imagination. It is not simply a matter of winning an argument or a contest of facts and frames. Because regenerativity requires a move away from the BAU mode of doing business, countering rationalizations involves more than the personal expression of values. To counter a rationalization is to propose something positive, to explore an innovative possibility. When this occurs at the organizational level, it involves cultural innovation though strong leadership. In the context of sustainability, strong leadership means modelling and supporting colleagues to engage in values-based conversations with greater confidence and clarity. Both Joost and Wouter regularly dedicate time and space to values-based conversations, embedding values in the business culture and decision-making. Wouter calls his main strategy for building a values-based culture "relentless execution". By practicing relentlessly, TSC's leadership builds ethical muscles for voicing both personal and corporate values. Over time, skillful values-based conversations become routinized organizational practices. Through the habitual expression of values, and the normalization of sustainability practices that build on those habits, TSC's regenerative business culture develops and is reproduced despite the many changing circumstances that the business contends with.

Exercises

Exercise 1   "Voice lessons"

I raise my voice – not so I can shout but so that those without a voice can be heard.

– Malala Yousafzi

Articulate the challenge: It is challenging in life to express our personal values and principles when the situation does not support such action; when we lack confidence or feel pressure to remain silent or to do nothing. In this exercise we take up this challenge and practice developing skills that help to voice our values in pragmatic ways.

Time: 10 minutes introduction and preparation. 5–10 minutes exercise per person

Purpose: The purpose is to help build confidence in our skills for expressing values in ways that do not systematically place us at a disadvantage. There is no need to be an idealist or a hero to voice our core concerns. For example, we can think that putting our values into words and actions can appear self-serving, that it turns us into "greenies" or "do-gooders", or we can feel that it separates us from our friends or colleagues. Such thoughts can act against developing our pragmatic skills for voicing.

What does this exercise make possible?

This exercise helps to build a toolbox of actions that open possibilities for voicing. There are different ways of starting a values-based conversation and this exercise explores those possibilities.

Opening invitation: Participants are invited to develop ways of thinking about their interior rationalizations and how these can be used to innovate pragmatic responses to ethical opportunities and challenges.

Materials and spaces:

The following multiple-choice questions can be used or, alternatively, participants can develop their own MCQs in their groups.

---

1. A new friend comes to you and complains bitterly about another friend of yours. What do you do?

    A. Say nothing to anyone and trust it all works out because you don't want to upset "things".
    B. Tell the other friend about the complaints.
    C. Discuss with the new friend that this complaining makes you uncomfortable.
    D. Discuss with all your friends how complaints are fine but be open and honest about them.

2. You work in a lighting store. Your boss tells you to always sell the old, stocked lights fitting before the new ones. Later, a customer asks, "Yes, I will buy this light but please give me the newest goods". You go out the back to get the item. What do you do?

    A. Sell them the new light and hope your boss does not find out.
    B. Tell the customer that all the lights are the same age.
    C. Discuss the whole thing with the boss and tell her how uncomfortable you feel about this.
    D. Get the old light fitting and think to yourself, "It won't hurt anyone to give them this older product".

3. You are a student and its midnight on the last night before a 2,000-word essay is due in the morning. The essay is for a course you need to complete to get your degree. You need a grade of 60% in the essay to pass the course. What do you do?

    A. Go to the GPT-4 website and type in the assignment instructions.
    B. Work through the night and get it done.
    C. Write an email to the lecturer saying that I am sick (you're not) and asking for an extension.
    D. Write an email to the lecturer explaining everything honestly and asking for an extension.

Participants can be provided with copies of the above MCQs, or they will need their own computers or materials if they develop their own MCQs. The exercise can be done onsite or online and suitable spaces should be organized to suit these options.

Group participation and configuration:

The exercise is best done in small groups of 3–4 participants. Each participant is expected to be present and focused and show respect and understanding toward each other. Preliminary instructions on listening skills, peer coaching, and creating supportive sharing environments might be provided beforehand.

Sequence of Steps and Time Allocation (1 hr 30 mins):

Step 1: Introduce the exercise with a discussion of rationalizations and their impact on expressing core values. (15 mins)

Step 2: In groups of three or four discuss the MCQ scenarios and the multiple-choice options or create your own options and think about why you made up these new responses. (10 mins)

Step 3: Discuss the possibility of options other than those provided to address the ethical dilemma in each MCQ. (10 mins)

Step 4: Discuss the pros and cons for each of the options (those provided and those created in the teams), decide on the most pragmatic options, and discuss why they are so. (10 mins)

Step 5: Based on your discussions from the above steps note down all the factors that characterize pragmatic responses to ethical dilemmas. (15 mins)

Step 6: Collate all the factors from each group (from Step 5) and discuss (30 mins)

Tips and Traps:

- The multiple steps mean that time facilitation is important.
- The list of pragmatic factors can be augmented by previous suggestions and the full set could be distributed to each participant.
- Introducing the exercise and discussing its purpose in advance of the group work is crucial for participant understanding and commitment to the exercise.

Variations:

- The exercise can be run online or onsite.
- The MCQ scenarios can be changed and adapted to the type and needs of the audience.
- The "Tale of Two Stories" exercise, included in the Appendices of Gentile's book *Giving Voice to Values*, could be done as an introduction to this exercise.

Exercise 2   "The GVV Freeze"

We are all very good at rationalizing our actions so that they are in line with our selfish motives.

– Dan Ariely

Articulate the challenge: To act regeneratively, we need to practice building our "voice muscles". To do that we need to think about the inhibiting arguments we might encounter from either ourselves or others. It is useful to practice developing the basic conversational elements of the rationalizations that could pop up and well-crafted enabling responses that move things forward. Practicing these basic elements helps in finding your voice in, what are often tense, situations, especially when you feel that you lack support, credibility of authority. The example in this chapter of the intern who chose to 'speak up' by writing an email is illustrative of this common dilemma. It can be daunting as a 'newbie' to express what is on one's mind in the work setting. In the following exercise, you get the chance to practice in a group with an exercise called the *GVV Freeze*. This exercise will help to build up participants' knowledge and confidence in countering rationalization in pragmatic and helpful ways.

Time: 2 hours

Purpose of the exercise: This is a role play exercise designed to help participants develop and practice GVV scripts for voicing values in the workplace. The purpose of this exercise is to practice building, analyzing, and engaging in conversations that support the expression of values.

What does this exercise make possible? The exercise makes it possible to develop and practice pragmatic and creative ways of countering arguments and reasons that might otherwise inhibit your capacity to express concerns and views that are important to you.

Structure of exercise: Preliminary introductory class. It is best that a class be held before the exercise to ensure that that class and all group members are familiar with the basic vocabulary of, for example, rationalizations (inhibiting arguments), enabling arguments, core values, allies, 'voice', values, and the 7 GVV pillars (see Glossary at the end of the volume for basic definitions). The exercise itself is best carried out in groups of 4–6 members in the following structure

1. Plenary session at the beginning to introduce participants to the exercise.
2. Group work session to develop the scenarios and GVV Freeze scripts.
3. Plenary session where groups perform their role-play and GVV freeze analysis.
4. Plenary session to end for discussion, lessons learned and feedback.

Materials and spaces: Participants will need to record a description of a scenario and document a conversation with an analysis of the rationalizations and enabling responses.

Group participation and configuration: Groups of 4–6 members. The facilitator should move between groups to facilitate each of the following steps.

Sequence of Steps and Time Allocation:

Step 1:   Present and describe a slide detailing each of the following steps. (5 minutes)

Step 2:   Break into groups of 4–6. Each group develops and records a brief (100-word) scenario where a protagonist is faced with a sustainability challenge. The scenario describes that the protagonist is new to the workplace but feels that they must say or do something to express their core values given the circumstances they are encountering. The scenario should involve roles for all group members, except for one member who will act as the "GVV commentator" during the role play. The GVV commentator reads out the scenario at the beginning of the role play. In developing the scenario provide enough background to ensure an audience understands: i) what is the dilemma?; ii) background on the organization; iii) how and why the ethical dilemma/opportunity arose; iv) what values are involved?; v) key stakeholders and how might they be affected. (20 mins)

Step 3a: Given the preceding scenario, groups develop a scripted conversation for all the characters based on the GVV concepts of, for example, inhibiting and enabling arguments, core values, allies, stakeholders' interests, and values, and some of the 7 GVV pillars. There should be roles for all groups members (apart from the GVV commentator). In developing the scripts think about the following: What likely rationalizations will the protagonist encounter? What is at stake for the protagonist? What are the protagonist's preferences and style of communicating? What is the most powerful and persuasive arguments the protagonist can make? What is the protagonist's personal and professional purpose? What are the basic categories that the rationalizations fall into? (20 mins)

Step 3b: Include in the script points where the GVV Commentator stops the action by saying "Freeze" and proceed to explain what is happing according to GVV concepts. After the explanation/GVV analysis, the GVV commentator restarts the role play with "Action". This freeze-action aspect of the exercise provides an opportunity for the group to demonstrate its understanding of the GVV process and its creativity in developing persuasive and pragmatic conversations to move people toward ethical solutions based on core values. (15 mins)

Step 4: All groups gather and perform their role plays. Include 5 mins for Q and A (allow 10 minutes per group).

Step 5: Wrap up and knowledge sharing. Plenary questions for participants to respond to:
- What are your personal and team reflections about the case?
- What insights have you and your team gained in performing this exercise?
- What recommendations arising from the analysis of the case can you give to other individuals involved in similar ethical dilemmas?
- What are the broader implications of the case for regenerative entrepreneurs?

Tips and Traps: Timing is difficult for this exercise so facilitators should circulate among groups and encourage punctuality.

Variations: Ideas for changing it to accommodate other possibilities, e.g., running it online or with adapting it to undergraduates, postgrads, executive education, or community.

Suggested extension materials: Reading, watching, podcasts, videos, articles, etc, to extend the participants experience and learning.

Case questions

The following questions present opportunities for analyzing this chapter from a GVV perspective. There were many ethical challenges faced by TSC and its founding entrepreneurs and these case questions explore how the GVV pillar of rationalizations can be used to address those challenges.

1. What rationalizations do TSC and its leaders encounter in establishing a new regenerative business?
2. Using the references listed below, identify the strategy categories that these rationalizations fall into, e.g., standard practice, materiality, locus of responsibility & loyalty.

   Anand, V., Ashforth, B. E., Joshi, M., & Martini, P. J. (2004). Business as usual: The acceptance and perpetuation of corruption in organizations. *The Academy of Management Executive, 18*(2), 39–55.

   Gentile, M. C. (2010). *Giving voice to values: How to speak your mind when you know what's right* (Chapter 8 Reasons and rationalizations). New Haven, CT: Yale University Press.

   Heath, J. (2008). Business ethics and moral motivation: A criminological perspective. *Journal of Business Ethics, 83*(4), 595–614.

3. What counterarguments and strategies do TSC and its leaders use to respond to these rationalizations?
4. What patterns or general principles can you identify in the ways that TSC and its leaders express these counterarguments and overcome the rationalizations?
5. What are your main learnings from the case of TSC for your ability to create positive change?

Further Resources

The Seaweed Company: https://www.theseaweedcompany.com/
Seaweed solutions for performance health wellbeing: https://www.feedand additive.com/seaweed-solutions-for-performance-health-wellbeing/
   Dr. Stefan Kraan, Chief Scientific Officer of Seaweed Company: https://www.youtube.com/watch?v=7zSaEO4-oEk

Note

1 "Blue farmers" is a term proposed by Joost to identify a new category of land-based farmers who use the "blue" power of the sea, for example, seaweed products, to support agricultural activities on land. For example, The Seaweed Company has identified seaweed blends that support crop farming through reducing harmful inputs and improving the health and well-being of animals.

References

Bonan, A., Canon, C., Pokraka, L., Detablan, T., Esteves, A., & McHardy, G. (Eds.). (2020). *Steward-Ownership: A Short Guidebook to Legal Frameworks*. Hamburg: Purpose Foundation (Purpose Stiftung gGmbH).

Flannery, T. (2017). *Sunlight and Seaweed: An Argument for How to Feed, Power and Clean Up the World*. Text Publishing.

Kanter, R. M. (1994). Collaborative advantage. *Harvard Business Review*, 72(4), 96–108.

Lipshaw, J. M. (2020). The false dichotomy of corporate governance platitudes. *Journal of Corporation Law*, 46(2), 345–384.

Raisher, J. (Ed.) (2022). *Steward Ownership*. Hamburg, Germany: Purpose Foundation.

Schnatterly, K., Gangloff, K. A., & Tuschke, A. (2018). CEO wrongdoing: A review of pressure, opportunity, and rationalization. *Journal of Management*, 44(6), 2405–2432. doi:10.1177/0149206318771177

The Seaweed Company. (2022). The story of *The Seaweed Company*. *Medium*. Retrieved from https://medium.com/@theseaweedcompany/the-story-of-the-seaweed-company-c764777c2594

The Seaweed Company. (2023). *Our Purpose*. The Seaweed Company [Online]. Retrieved from https://www.theseaweedcompany.com/our-impact

Thomas, V. (2023). *Risk and Resilience in the Era of Climate Change*. New York: Palgrave Macmillan.

Yong, W. T. L., Thien, V. Y., Rupert, R., & Rodrigues, K. F. (2022). Seaweed: A potential climate change solution. *Renewable and Sustainable Energy Reviews*, *159*, 112222.

7

GIVING VOICE TO A
REGENERATIVE FUTURE

In this concluding chapter we weave together the core findings and insights derived from our four illustrative cases of regenerative organizations and their entrepreneurial leaders. Before doing that, we will recapitulate the main purpose of the book and emphasize the global contexts and conditions that make regenerative business such an important topic for sustainability and entrepreneurship studies. After this, we will discuss the core themes that run through the book and describe what insights have emerged from the chapters. This chapter is intended to be a source of inspiration for readers who wish to dig further into the entrepreneurial opportunities afforded by a regenerative perspective. We hope this chapter will stimulate further discussion on the challenging task of developing regenerative organizations. Sustainability is a multilevel affair that engages with personal, organizational, industry, national, and international levels of economic and workplace activity. If regenerative sustainability is our goal, then we will only get there through communicating and putting into practice those values that will guide us toward regenerative business

DOI: 10.4324/9781003330660-7

futures. In this chapter we discuss key dynamics in that process of holding and expressing our core values and we describe some of the personal- and enterprise-level factors that support a values-based movement toward regenerative sustainability.

Recapitulation

It is important to recognize that regenerative sustainability involves transformations in each of the environmental, social, and economic spheres of human activity. However, because of the scale of the impact of economic activity on the environment, and its pivotal importance for social health and well-being, the environmental domain needs special prioritization for action. There are four environmental sustainability imperatives challenging governments, businesses, and institutions to undertake significant transformation (Sachs et al., 2019). These imperatives are: i) the accelerating impact on the natural limits of the planet caused by economic consumption and production, ii) the worsening climate change crisis, iii) the collapse of biodiversity, and iv) the looming problem of biophysical tipping points. None of these challenges is being adequately addressed (Brovkin et al., 2021; Rockström & Gaffney, 2021). On the contrary, as these challenges go unmet, the need for more dramatic efforts and more forceful government regulation increases. At the firm level, a similar stepping up of sustainability aspirations is also required. But it is no longer sufficient to set net zero GHG emissions as the final goal, or to be satisfied with the conservation of what remains of crucial biophysical systems.

The significance of Earth Overshoot Day appearing earlier and earlier every year (for 2023 it is July 27) is that the power of the Earth to regenerate itself, to replenish its ecological and biophysical resilience, continues to be diminished by the extractive economic systems that characterize the Anthropocene epoch. Within a very brief period, humanity needs to turn this around and convert extractive systems into regenerative economies if it is to return the global system into something like "a safe and just operating space" (Raworth, 2012). This, in turn, needs regenerative business strategies to revive and restore the core planetary processes that create a stable and resilient Earth system. These daunting facts can elicit maladaptive responses that actively thwart constructive attempts to doing things differently. The immensity of the task of diverting a global trajectory can result in inaction and avoidance and even active denial of the basic problems. Some business leaders, however, see this urgent challenge also as an opportunity for innovation.

In the preceding chapters we investigated four diverse cases of regenerative organizations and their founding and leading entrepreneurs. We looked at the characteristics of these entrepreneurs' regenerative values, how they are expressed and how they build organizational climates that support others in voicing their values. Inspiring cases like these organizations are needed to turn the unusual into the ordinary, to shift our ambitions so that what is now uncommon can become the default, and, hence, to radically step up our expectations for what a sustainable organization and a responsible business might look like. We adopted an appreciative perspective on these cases and the entrepreneurs involved to identify ways of accelerating the pace at which we transition toward more sustaining forms of economic activity. We delved deeply into some of the micro-foundational practices that accompany regenerative renewal. What these organizations are doing is real and impactful and, while more research needs to be done on the exact outcomes being achieved, it is important to recognize that deep change in a positive direction is possible.

In the rest of this chapter, we highlight the most important findings from our case insights for creating and maintaining regenerative organizations from a values-based perspective. First, we will consider contributions of our case analyses to regenerative sustainability at the organizational level. Next, we will describe and discuss the key insights for supporting regenerative entrepreneurship. Third, we will briefly mention the contributions of our findings for the field of business ethics in general and GVV in particular. Fourth, we conclude this chapter with some comments on the future of regenerative sustainability and its relationship with business ethics education.

Insights into regenerative organizations

Regenerative organizations are at the forefront of sustainability transitioning. However, as we have seen from our diverse group of cases, they exist and operate within a broad spectrum of environments, from the market-based environments of international business to online community education settings. This broad selection of regenerative initiatives reflects: i) the diversity of responses that organizations and entrepreneurs are engaging in toward the global sustainability imperative; and ii) the shared values that those responses exhibit and enact as these organizations pave the way for other creative companies and community organizations to follow. In the introduction to this chapter, we mentioned some of the definitive qualities of these shared perspectives and the following section elaborates further on these commonalities. We pull together some of the key themes and learnings from our cases and develop frameworks for explaining why and how regenerative entrepreneurs enact their values in the organizations they lead.

Sustainability-as-flourishing

The sustainability-as-flourishing perspective reframes the value base of establishing and running a business. All the cases could be seen to exemplify this perspective in their own ways. Most importantly, all showed that sustainability-as-flourishing involved the expression of core values. Values of compassion through collaboration, of integrity through how people and nature are valued, of honesty through communication with stakeholders were all seen as fundamental to the purpose of the organization. The area where sustainability-as-flourishing was most evident was in the prioritization of values. A key feature of each of our illustrative cases of regenerative business is that they hold, both implicitly in their values and explicitly in their decision-making, an embedded sustainability model (see Figure 6.2 in the previous chapter). That is, they prioritize social-ecological purposes over economic ones. This means that a critical social tipping point has been reached within the governance and purpose of regenerative organizations. That tipping point is the movement from seeing profit as the goal of business and organizational life to profit as the means and people and planet as the goal. This core feature of regenerativity means that the financial aspects of organizations, whether for-profit corporations, for-purpose enterprises, or community organizations, are regarded as means for benefiting human communities and the ecological systems on which they depend rather than the goal. Regenerative businesses flip the prioritization of organizational purposes to place social-ecological purposes as the guiding context for making money. Money is not left behind in this radical reframing of purpose. In fact, the economic realities of organizational life take on a more integrated and socially embedded role.

Regenerative organizations will plan and develop strategies to make money but not at the cost compromising their social-ecological purposes and goals. If their social-ecological services or products are not financially viable, they will innovate until they find a solution that does follow the embedded model. The perspective of sustainability-as-flourishing supports regenerative organizations in achieving their financial goals, and to do so without compromising their social and environmental values and priorities. This is precisely what we see in our cases. Making money becomes a means for the expression of core values and not at the cost of those values. Hence, rationalizations that pit the profit motive against the social-ecological motive are concretely defused.

Interdependency and complexity/systems thinking

Regenerative organizations see sustainability as a constellation of interdependent factors that reinforce each other. An example of this is the common view that the creative possibilities for technical and social innovation are stimulated, rather than inhibited by, the recognition of environmental limits. Embracing social-ecological realities, for example, the interconnectedness of the nine planetary processes and the 17 SDGs, generates creative business solutions. Complexity and system thinking capacities support a both/ and approach to providing answers to sustainability challenges. These skills constitute one of the fundamental competencies for sustainable business management (Wesselink, Blok, van Leur, Lans, & Dentoni, 2015). Competent sustainability managers, consultants, and policy makers must be able to analyze and work with systems, their sub-units, their interdependency, feedback loops, and scale effects. Recognizing such interdependencies and systemic complexities means that values take on a more prominent role in decision-making. Although data always plays a crucial role in decision-making, no amount of information analysis ever provides a clear pathway for navigating the wickedly complex problems that businesses encounter in their sustainability strategies. Our cases show that regenerative businesses rely on core values plus information to navigate through this process. From this interdependency perspective, the creativity needed to introduce new sustainability-oriented products and services is intimately connected with ethical innovation and with the embedded personal and organizational capacity to communicate and explore values in skilful and useful ways.

Real value and regenerative sustainability

An entrepreneur is someone who creates new forms of value. A regenerative entrepreneur is someone who creates new forms of "*real* value", that is, value that benefits people and the ecological systems they depend on (Sternad, Kennelly, & Bradley, 2016) while generating the financial means to do that. Creating financial value that does not result in social-ecological benefits is not sustainable value and may even be value-destroying (Edwards, Benn, & Starik, 2017). Destructive value is financial or monetary value that is created to the detriment of vulnerable human communities, endangered biological ecosystems, and crucial planetary geophysical processes. This distinction between regenerative or "real" value and unsustainable value is a crucial one that our cases have highlighted. Referring to Figure 1.2, unsustainable or destructive value lies outside the "safe and just operating space for humanity". Financial value created at the cost of the social floor, or the environmental ceiling is unsustainable.

Based on this model and using the language of political economist Joseph Schumpeter, we can distinguish between two kinds of entrepreneuring – creative destruction and, what we call, destructive creation. *Creative destruction* is a common term in economics and entrepreneurship studies. However, in the context of our study of regenerativity, we focus its definition to relate specifically to the innovation of sustainability-oriented products and services that move economies into the safe (environmentally sustainable) and just (socially sustainable) operating space (see Figure 1.2 and the section on Doughnut Economics in Chapter 1). Creative destruction enables social and environmental sustainability and it disrupts and disables (destroys) the unsustainable and extractive alternatives. In contrast, *destructive creation* (Mazzucato, 2013; Soete, 2013) is that form of business innovation that undermines a "safe and just operating space". Destructive creation is Business-As-Usual (BAU) innovation that seeks profit as the cost of social and environmental harms. Entrepreneuring as creative destruction disrupts and reshapes BAU entrepreneuring to create real value. Destructive creation is innovation that benefits a few at the expense of the many with social and environmental impact that reduces the resilience and well-being of natural and human systems. Our cases provide evidence that the values systems underpinning these two visions of entrepreneuring are vastly different. The values that inform creative destruction and the stewarding of real value are characteristic of regenerative businesses and the entrepreneurs that build and manage them.

Regenerative values support organizations to move beyond destructive creation (BAU innovation), whose goal is limited to financial value, to achieve a deeper and more sustaining forms of real value in business. Regenerative entrepreneurs create new forms of real value, not only by diminishing the harm done to people and ecological systems, but also by the restorative impacts their businesses have in supporting the regeneration of social-ecological systems. Traditional businesses create financial value through the instrumentalization of people, as human resources, and ecosystems, as natural resources. This is extractive profit and, while it may create immense amounts of wealth for some and increase financial wealth for many, it comes at the cost of the resilience and health of the social-ecological systems that are the foundation for that wealth. For regenerative entrepreneurs, founding their organizations is a way to voice their values in ways that make a creative difference.

Imagination and ethical innovation

Imagination lies at the heart of all innovation and true creativity. Business innovation requires more than that, but no innovation occurs with creative experimentation of possibility. From a GVV perspective, ethics and the expression of core values is also essentially a creative process of taking hold of opportunities and responding to confronting challenges in inventive ways. The cases revealed many instances where individuals and their organizations displayed their capacities for breaking out of BAU habits and acting with imagination. This ability for imaginative action was present in the communications and conversations that form the basis of many of the illustrative examples provided in the cases. We saw that by giving voice to regenerative prioritizations, values, and purpose, stakeholders gained trust in the regenerative visions communicated by the business founders and leaders. At the same time, it is interesting to note that space was also created for stakeholders, such as employees, local communities, and natural systems, to voice their own needs and expectations. Of special relevance here is the role of listening to the "voice" of nature and of local ecosystems. Listening is a core requirement of deep communication, and this is especially true of those stakeholders who lack a voice, or established power mechanisms to express their values and concerns (Gentile, 2016).

Empowerment and virtuous and vicious circles

A shared feature of regenerative organizations evident from the cases is the empowerment of "voice" among stakeholders, where "voice" refers to the capacity of a stakeholder to express their concerns, ideas, and creative suggestions and values. With this empowerment, regenerative organizations can be vehicles for voicing core values and visions of sustainability-as-flourishing. Consequently, the organizations described here are functionally acting as sites for human development and community renewal. The case of The Seaweed Company (TSC) demonstrates this process of empowering voice at multiple levels in both its internal and external relations. By building a corporate culture that enables stakeholder voice, TSC creates conditions for a positive, or virtuous, cycle where organizational values are reaffirmed and the opportunities for voicing are reinforced. One of the 12 assumptions of the GVV approach is that, as Gentile puts it, "The more I believe it is possible to voice and act on my values, the more likely I will be to do so" (Gentile, 2010, p. 74). In contrast, a corporate culture that silences voice, that creates workplace environments where the lack of psychological safety works against the empowerment of stakeholders can create a negative (or vicious) cycle, where the voice is weakened, and organizational values are diluted. Figure 7.1 describes the contrasting phases of virtuous and vicious cycles of empowering and disempowering voice, respectively.

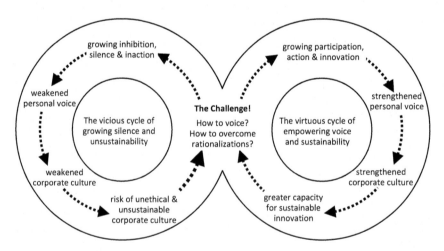

Figure 7.1 Voice and rationalization as virtuous & vicious circles of corporate culture.

The figure describes the process of initially responding to "the sustainability challenge" and the requisite capacity to voice and overcome rationalizations. Depending on the response, there is either a growing participation in voicing, ethical action, and innovation or the opposite in growing inhibition, silence, and inaction on sustainability issues. Individual responses aggregate or co-create either weakened or strengthened corporate culture for voicing. The macro level of culture interacts with the micro level of the individual to either enable or inhibit individual voice. The voice-enabling culture of regenerative organizations supports the virtuous cycle in this process.

Insights into regenerative entrepreneurship

Technology, nature-based solutions, and the intergenerational perspective

Like all contemporary organizations, regenerative organization require technologies such as Communication and Information Technology (CIT) to function effectively. However, regenerative sustainability solutions place technology at the service of benefits to nature and communities rather than at the service of short-term efficiency, cost cutting, or improving profit margins. When CIT and technological innovations are seen primarily as efficiency measures, they can result in rebound effects where resource use and pollution go up rather than down (Kunkel & Tyfield, 2021). From a regenerative perspective, the adoption of technological solutions works best when they are regarded as means for achieving social-ecological benefits rather than for micro-economic efficiencies. We saw this in the work of TSC and their view of seaweed as a natural technology that can provide long-term benefits to local communities and the natural systems they depend on. An illustration of this intergenerational perspective comes from one of our interviewees, Wouter Zwagemakers, Head of Commerce at The Seaweed Company. Wouter told us that he had written a letter to his children, to their future selves:

> I wrote a letter to my kids, for when they're eighteen. I said guys, I've been doing quite a lot of reflection work, soul searching work. I found that my sweet spot is in nature technology and foods ... I like making and supporting systemic changes, holistic changes. I actually wrote all this stuff in a letter to them; I hope they open it when they're eighteen.

This intergenerational perspective is a fundamental driver of the motivational energy and creativity that informs the entrepreneurs we interviewed for this book. The regenerative perspective is one that sees any kind of innovation, be it a technologically or nature-based solution, within the context of intergenerational sustainability. While intergenerational awareness by itself is not sufficient to result in successful business or community innovation, without it, no regenerative outcomes are possible.

Entrepreneurship as enabling societal change

Like other entrepreneurs, our regenerative leaders exemplify the importance of personal fulfilment in pursuing their work. What is different with our cases is the personal sense of contribution is so intimately connected to their regenerative business vision. To put it another way, our regenerative entrepreneurs are undertaking a process of emancipation, both externally, in their professional journey, and internally, in their personal life (Rindova, Barry, & Ketchen, 2009). The development of the Inner Development Goals (IDGs) to complement the work of the UN Sustainable Development Goals (SDGs) is reflective of this move toward more interior, values-based views on sustainability transitioning.

The English word entrepreneur comes directly from the French and means 'one who undertakes'. It is a deliberate journey that navigates between the potential for personal development and the external opportunities for achieving organizational goals. In this sense, the entrepreneurs considered here are building regenerative lives as well as regenerative organizations and, just as importantly, they want their organization to support that journey for other people. The Humanium Metal (HM) case is a good illustration of this feature. HM sees its work as a vehicle for regenerating communities caught in the crisis of gun violence. HM's business model might be thought of as a kind of regenerative circularity in that it recycles the stuff of violence into the possibility of personal and community development. While HM aims to do more by way of environmental sustainability at the level of product development, the regeneration of peaceful human community ultimately restores natural systems as part of that journey.

The entrepreneurs in the organizations presented here are often regarded by their members as vehicles for effecting macro-level, systemic change. Combining the lens of micro, meso, and macro leverage points

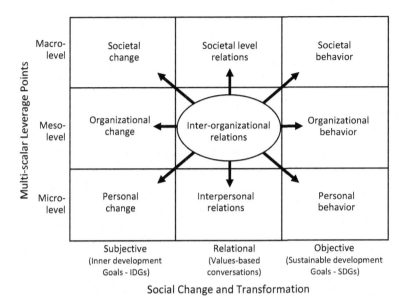

Figure 7.2 The sweet spot of societal change.

(cf. Meadows, 2009) with the dynamic of inner-outer development results in a framework that sheds light on entrepreneurs' motivations for effecting social change. Inner-outer development, as represented by the IDGs and SDGs respectively, is a function of human relations, dialogue, and conversation (see Figure 7.2). The communication of values, goals, and purposes provides a basis for all inner and outer growth. This relational domain of social change and transformation informs and motivates the development of both the inner life of mindsets, feelings, and imagination and the outer life of social behavior, work, education, and community life. Where the meso level of organization is a means for scaling up personal and organization impacts to the systems level of society, the relational world of communication and conversation is a pivotal domain for linking inner change with outer action. Consequently, the relational domain of organizational communication and action in community and in the marketplace can be understood as the "sweet spot" for scaling up regenerative impacts.

This is precisely why our regenerative entrepreneurs placed so much importance on the role of values-based conversations (the relational level) with all members of their extended circle of stakeholders and why they build their (the meso-level) businesses and enterprises to act as vehicles for those conversations. It was a repeated theme in the interviews that regenerative entrepreneurs purposefully aim for societal-level change and transformation through leveraging this "sweet spot" for change and transformation. They see their organizations as means for "voicing" their values with the purpose of scaling up their impact on societal sustainability transitions.

In founding their organizations, regenerative entrepreneurs empower themselves to impact on, and interact with, sustainability futures on multiple levels. Organizations enable people to express their values through their work in collaboration with other stakeholders. This meso-level engagement impacts on society but also provides a vehicle for stakeholders to give "voice" to their dreams at the personal level. As JP described the impact of Earth Regenerators on its members,

> People were thrilled to meet each other from across the world. Who, you know, share the same values very much. So, we care deeply about the earth. We care deeply about the loss of relationality and rebuilding that. So many people are disconnected from where [they live]. They want to find their place and be of service to the Earth in that place.

Because the goal of regenerative sustainability creates opportunities for deep change in both mindsets and systems, it can have therapeutic impacts on individuals, groups, and communities. Regenerativity, as an aspirational goal, moves organizations, even in the case here of the privately owned for-profit, into functioning as a site for social-ecological development.

Entrepreneurship and integrity

Chapter 2 presented a model of values alignments and misalignments between individual stakeholders and the organizations they worked for or interacted with (see Figure 2.2). Personal and organizational integrity can be regarded as the process of minimizing these gaps and misalignments in values. Integrity is fundamentally the capacity to express core values across different social situations. For example, the values that underpin the prioritization of social-ecological benefits will be expressed even when financial constraints are experienced. Rather than closing off opportunities, however, this kind of values-based integrity creates the possibility for innovation and doing things in new ways. A definitive feature of regenerative entrepreneurs is that they are sensitive to situations which place pressure on the integrity of their values-based decision-making and where values are muted or even silenced. In such situations, there can be misalignments between personal and organizational expressions of values and between current and future aspirations. We saw in several instances that regenerative organizations and their leaders are aware of the importance of these alignments and that they develop strategies for ensuring integrity, such as modelling and communicating regenerative values, recruitment practices and stakeholder communications.

Regenerative leadership

Regenerative entrepreneurs are business leaders who innovate to help heal the economic, social, and environmental harms caused by the commercial activities based of the extractive economies of unsustainable government and business activities. As economist Kate Raworth describes it, "the degenerative industrial system" (2020) is based on a linear take–make–use–lose approach to commercial activity. Profits are maximized by externalizing (hiding) the true costs of extractive production–consumption exchanges. BAU understandings of sustainability leadership do not share the values or the special prioritization of values that regenerativity logically demands. To move toward authentic, intergenerational sustainability, a more ambitious understanding and practical implementation of sustainability is required. The values that underpin this new perspective on leadership are not necessarily unusual; what is different is the circle of reach in which they are applied. For example, values of respect and compassion for people and nature are extended outwards to include not only stakeholders in supply and demands networks but all living systems. Regenerative leadership extends this circle of ethical embrace to deliberately connect and integrate what extractive businesses assumes to be divided and disconnected (Hutchins & Storm, 2019). Regenerativity integrates the human worlds of business and economics with the world of nature and geophysical landscape. Regenerative mindsets aim to complement social sustainability and diversity perspective and practices with environmental sustainability and nature-based perspectives and practices (see Landrum, 2018). Regenerative leaders display traits that connect emotion with scientific rationality and institutional logic. Finally, we see in the work of the regenerative leaders portrayed here that vision and aspirational is connected directly with the world of strategic action and performance.

Regenerative and the embedded perspective

For the entrepreneurs and organizational leaders depicted in the preceding chapters, nature has an intrinsic value. They see themselves and their ventures as embedded in natural systems rather than purely social or economic systems that are independent of the natural world. Consequently, the values they hold to guide their business activities emphasize that connectedness. They see natural systems as key stakeholders and prioritize the value and creative insights that are generated through respecting and listening to nature. In this way, regenerative entrepreneurs collaborate with nature and the local, traditional, and indigenous communities that are close to nature. This embeddedness is a distinctive feature of regenerative mindsets and clearly distinguishes regenerative from conventional forms of organizing. This embeddedness has a specific meaning in that economic goals are means for achieving social and environmental goals. An entrepreneur's own sense of social-ecological embeddedness feeds into the regenerative qualities (see Chapter 1) of sustainability-as-flourishing, the pursuit of real value, nature-inspired innovation, and social empowerment. All these are held within an intergenerational sense of responsibility and commitment.

Regenerative and extractive entrepreneuring

It is not all forms of human economic activity that are driving the multiple social and environmental crises occurring around the world. A large majority of the world population, about 84%, or 6.7 billion people, live on less than $30 per day (Roser, 2021). The "Great Acceleration" studies (Brolin & Kander, 2022; Steffen, Broadgate, Deutsch, Gaffney, & Ludwig, 2015; Wiedmann, Lenzen, Keyßer, & Steinberger, 2020) show that it is affluence and technology and not population growth that are the main drivers of resource use. It is not the economic systems of indigenous communities, traditional agriculture, or subsistence farming that is behind the environmental crises of climate change, biodiversity loss, water pollution, or land use change. The problem lies with the narrow application and pursuit of values that underpin extractive systems of market capitalism, entrepreneurialism, and economic growth. This "extractive economy" (Fullerton, 2015) and accompanying forms of extractive entrepreneurialism drive unsustainable modes of commercial activity.

It is not that extractive entrepreneuring is driven by a completely separate set of core values and that these values should be muted in favor of more generative ones. The values that underpin wealth creation, employment, innovation, and technological invention are not bad or morally inferior. Rather, the problem is that these values are pursued and incentivised in an extraordinarily narrow manner. Extractive values are not essentially different from regenerative values but are focused on a much narrower set of stakeholders, timeframes, and success indicators. The well-being of owners, shareholders, and financial investors are prioritized over those social and natural stakeholders that are the foundation of that wealth. The financial signals of the market are prioritized over the scientific signals of ecological and biophysical degradation, social inequality, and economic risk. The entrepreneurs represented here each demonstrate how a more expansive and, consequently, more inclusive application of values open new entrepreneurial avenues for truly sustainable forms of organizing and doing business. From this perspective, regenerative entrepreneuring is not a niche form of sustainability-oriented innovation fit for a specialized group of actors at the margins of the economy. It is extractive forms of entrepreneuring that exclude and marginalize through narrow application of values and narrow understanding of what is of value. In contrast, regenerative entrepreneuring seeks to broaden the circle of wealth and value creation to include ecological wealth, community resilience, and human well-being with a more inclusive circle of stakeholders over extended timeframes.

Regenerative values and the Anthropocene

There are three general points we see repeatedly emerging in these cases in the relationship between entrepreneurial values and the challenges of the Anthropocene. First, values guide us toward our core goals and regenerative values will guide us toward the goals for a safe and just Anthropocene. In the epoch of the Anthropocene, our core business goals can no longer be concerned primarily with economic values. Business goals must not only include social and environmental goals but prioritize them. It is still the case that the responsibility of business is to "increase its profits so long as it stays within the rules of the game … without deception or fraud" as Milton Friedman puts it. But the rules of the game have changed, and it is a new kind of game that businesses need to play. Even Milton Friedman admitted that profits must be pursued "while conforming to their basic rules of the society, both those embodied in law and those embodied in ethical custom" (Friedman, 1970, p. 173). If those rules, laws, values, and customs change because of emerging challenges, even according to Friedman, the basic responsibilities of business must also change. Many corporate economies are larger than many national economies. Across many parts of the world – East, West, North and South – the physical and social power of business to transform landscape and communities is much greater than that of the political systems of those communities. Along with that immense power comes great responsibility but also the possibility of doing business in ways that engages a wider variety of values and motivations.

Second, while values can be expressed and prioritized by different cultures, communities, and organizations in distinctive and even incompatible ways, humans across the world share a set of core values that agreements such as the United Nations Declaration on Human Rights attest to. Great differences in priorities and preferences exist but even in the face of those differences people have found ways to morally connect, to persuade others of their distinctive views, and to resonate with the deep purposes that can often be discovered through creativity and dialogue. This is particularly true when different communities face the same challenges and threats, which is precisely the case with current global problems. Values, and their application in business to meet the challenge of regenerativity, can empower cross-cultural solidarity and collective action.

Third, expressing values in the pragmatic world of business is intimately coupled with innovation. Drawing on the work of Albert Hirschman (1970), Mary Gentile proposes that facing up to ethical challenges can be boiled down to three choices. Two of these options, to leave the situation or to remain in the situation and be silent, do nothing to systematically resolve the ethical challenge. Exiting or remaining silent are not particularly creative ways of facing up to values-based challenges, nor are they likely to bring about positive change. For a global challenge such as climate change, the choice of exiting might be the solution according to Elon Musk and his SpaceX initiative and the choice of remaining silent might be the choice of Big Oil. Neither of these options faces up to the realities of human impacts on human communities and the Earth's living biosphere. It is the third option, to remain with the challenge and to creatively express one's core values, that opens avenues for lasting change. It is in choosing to transform organizations through collaborative invention that the real opportunities will emerge. This is where the deep connections between innovation and values begin to show themselves. To move toward regenerative sustainability, entrepreneurs develop competencies in adaptive systems thinking, in the management of interpersonal relations, in strategic skills and planning, in technical and financial skills, and in anticipatory and visioning skills. Most of all, however, we see with our regenerative entrepreneurs, the central role played by regenerative values and the normative domain of ethical competencies in building organization that are fit-for-purpose for the 21st century.

Regenerative entrepreneurs are not heroes

Our final insight into the nature of regenerative entrepreneuring is that this style of sustainability leadership is not about being a hero. The men and women described here are very professional people who act to build and manage their organizations in pragmatic and quietly determined ways. Practice, skill, commitment, and life experience are all involved but these are ordinary qualities possessed by ordinary people. At the organizational level, a regenerative enterprise is also not about being a heroic organization. We have seen that very normal companies and communities can find everyday means to express their values in powerful and persuasive ways. Though this book specifically explores the voicing of values of regenerative entrepreneurs, it is important to recognize that voicing values is not something only regenerative entrepreneurs can do. They are not ethical celebrities with special Giving Voice to Values 'superpowers'. No one knows how to voice their values from the start, nor is it something that only certain people can learn. Rather, finding your voice is something that anyone can do, through practice and intrapreneurship, through pragmatic intent. One especially interesting element of the stories told here is that people involved in regenerative business seem to be having lots of fun. While difficulties and obstacles are clearly also part of the journey, being involved in a regenerative enterprise is socially engaging and personally rewarding on many levels – professionally, emotionally, and morally.

Insights into Giving Voice to Values

Giving Voice to Values and taking hold of ethical opportunities

So, what new insights into Giving Voice to Values (GVV) have been gained in the process of looking at these four cases? One pattern that comes through very forcefully from each of these stories is that GVV is not only about voicing values in reaction to ethical problems. It is also about taking hold of ethical opportunities. Our cases demonstrate the power of expressing values as an opportunity to regenerate the Earth and foster the transition toward a sustainable future. Initiatives such as the 4-Returns Framework are the organizational equivalent of a skilful communication of values that can empower, encourage, and inspire others. During times of crisis, it is natural to feel overwhelmed and uncertain about the future. However, they can also be framed as opportunities to reassess priorities and realize new visions of the future. Our entrepreneurs discover and create opportunities in interesting ways. They stay up to date with the latest trends in the field of regenerative business, they look for the development of social practices that can support personal growth and organizational transformation, and they continuously identify emerging opportunities for collaboration and connecting with local communities. Framing ethical challenges as opportunities for renewal and innovation lies at the heart of regenerative entrepreneuring. In addition to operating with all the economic and regulatory challenges of conventional commercial and community environments, regenerative businesses are characterized by their creativity in turning the challenge of global environmental crises into opportunities for innovation.

GVV and the spectrum of ethical action

Let us continue with this insight that GVV is about grasping opportunity as much as responding to problems. The notion of 'voice' in the GVV approach to ethics is a metaphor for all the personal and collective avenues by which people express themselves. To voice can be to contribute ideas, express criticisms, articulate creative suggestions and dreams, or, alternatively, it can be to communicate concerns, take oppositional standpoints, and provide evidence of wrongdoing. To voice means to be free and to feel free to say what is in one's heart and on one's mind. Voicing values or not does not only relate to meeting ethical challenges but to taking hold of ethical opportunities. In many ways, silence, and inaction in the face of ethical opportunities, might be the biggest ethical problem that the global environmental crisis has made apparent. Silence in the face of ethical problems allows unethical action and toxic cultures to grow and become systemic. But silence as a response to ethical opportunity denies hope, stops growth and development, and cuts short possibilities for change. Recognizing, or framing, the opportunity dimension of ethical action opens new worlds of possibility for expressing voice and for analysing the factors that can either support or suppress voice.

The following table explores this extension of the GVV approach to include the notion of a spectrum of interpretive lenses or "frames" for responding to problems, opportunities, and everything in between. A frame is an activity schema that helps to make sense of an event. Adopting a different frame can create a new understanding and/or a new mode of practice. The spectrum of ethical framing is the continuum of responses ranging from reactive to proactive. To this point GVV has focused on the skilful voicing of values in reaction to, or as a response to, moral challenges and we complement that with the notion of proactive framings to highlight ethical opportunities. Reactively voicing values in response to emerging global crises is an important dimension of ethical action in that it helps to reinforce ethical capacities and to safeguard against the corruption of values. To this point, the GVV approach to business ethics has focused on dealing with ethical problems. It has provided guidance on what to do when actors want to express their ethical commitments in response to situations that corrupt or harm.

But what if there is nothing imminently problematic, no ethical obstacle, or moral hazard present other than that the chance to do things differently goes unexpressed and overlooked. For example, one of the big ethical challenges that we face in the world of business today is not that businesses go about harming people and nature but that they do not take up the positive opportunity for helping people and nature to flourish. The banality of this BAU world of uncritical and mechanical acceptance of the status quo needs to be disrupted and exposed. Businesses, their owners, managers, and stockholders are missing the immense business opportunities for transforming BAU business models. In contrast, the organizations and entrepreneurs looked at here in our cases are taking hold of prospects others do not see. They are proactively seizing opportunities and not only acting against the unsustainable practices that surround them. This concept of creating or discovering *ethical opportunity* has not been explored enough in theories of business ethics or entrepreneurship.

Table 7.1 combines three frames – problem–opportunity, voice–silence and personal–organizational. Each of these frames represents a spectrum of possibilities rather than a dichotomy of discreet opposites. For example, voice is not only an ethical capacity possessed by individuals but also a collective capacity that can be evident in the actions of dyads, small groups, teams, decision-making committees, organizations, and even larger collectives. Similarly, the lens of voice–silence covers an infinite range of actions, ranging from complete silence and inaction to modest levels of voice and behavior to powerful displays of ethical voice and action. The moral act of voicing values can occur both when facing ethical problems *and* when

Table 7.1 Challenges and opportunities: new ways of framing voice

		Challenges	Opportunities
The personal domain	**Voicing personal values**	Speaking up against the challenge of ethical hazards and unethical activities	Speaking up to create ethical opportunities and innovative possibilities
	Silencing personal values	Silence and inaction against ethical challenges and unethical activities	Missing opportunities to voice values and silencing possibilities for creative action
The organizational domain	**Voicing organizational values**	An organizational culture of voice in the face of unethical activities becomes normalized	An organizational culture of innovation and grasping opportunities to voice values
	Silencing organizational values	An organizational culture of silence in response to unethical activities and global challenges	A BAU organizational culture of missed opportunities, lack of creativity and innovation

opportunities emerge. Ethical silence can similarly occur in the face of both these circumstances. Silence and lack of vision in taking up opportunities for ethical action is particularly pernicious when the status quo itself is toxic, unethical, and silences core values. The minimalist BAU approach to sustainability is problematic because it is so widely accepted as good enough. The cases discussed here are intriguing because they illustrate how many opportunities go begging. The opportunities for regenerative sustainability are so many and so economically valuable and yet they go unnoticed by conventional businesses. To give but one example, the preservation and rejuvenation of the biosphere is an area rich in global business opportunities (as the TSC and Commonland cases demonstrate) and yet these market possibilities are hardly recognised by conventional corporations. They show so clearly that the BAU economy is not taking up the ethical challenge of doing business in a way that benefits the long-term prosperity of people and the natural systems they depend on.

The key point behind Table 7.1 is that, in the domain of personal and collective voice, proactive possibilities and opportunities for expressing values need to be recognized as much as obvious instances of speaking up against existing unethical actions and events. The lack of action in taking up regenerative opportunities is one of the most urgent ethical and sustainability challenges facing communities across the world. The regenerative businesses and entrepreneurs presented here provide powerful and instructive examples of how these opportunities can be taken hold of in creative and inspiring ways.

Conclusion – The future of regenerative sustainability

Regenerative business models are a glimpse into the future of how mainstream businesses can operate. They offer a tangible vision of how sustainable approaches to economic development can align economic needs with the needs of people and planet. But how will this regenerative alternative become the default? How will the transition to regenerativity become the preferred approach to working with organizational sustainability? Nancy Landrum has written on how a regenerative business, "looks beyond growth and consumption, integrates environmental and ecological science, and adopts practices to repair the damage of the industrial consumer economy" (Landrum, 2018, p. 302). This approach to doing business and to forming organizations seems very distant from the mainstream of contemporary society and yet the cases described here show that it is not only possible, but remarkably evident that regenerative organizations are being founded and successfully developed.

Many actors will play a role in the emergence of regenerative businesses, communities, and economies. Responsible governments will have their part to play in establishing the regulatory environments that support the emergence of regenerative organizations. Entrepreneurs will be crucial because they will materialize the immense opportunities of regenerative enterprise and inspire other to do similarly. Investors are key actors in this transition and the emergence of a new culture of regenerative investment will be central to the development of a regenerative economy. The need for businesses investment that focuses on the restoration and regeneration of human communities and the natural systems they depend on is increasingly evident. There are huge economic opportunities here for those that can see that sustainability is not a marginal issue in business but is the central business issue of 21st century. Investment entrepreneurs are needed who recognize that the only value creation that will have any worth in the future is value built on environmental regeneration, community resilience, and economic responsibility. The power and impact of human organizations have become too great for anything less. Consumers also have their role to play but the core factors for initiating regenerative transitions will lie in entrepreneurial vision and practice. The future of regenerative sustainability can be closely tied to the success of regenerative entrepreneurship. As we face increasing environmental challenges such as climate change, resource depletion, and biodiversity loss, our current economic markets, models, and regulatory mechanisms are still based on BAU mindsets that marginalise ambitious forms of sustainability like regenerativity. Similarly, we face multiple social challenges, such as inequality, conflicts over land and natural resources, which are deeply connected to environmental issues. Expressing human and environmental values is an important ingredient in how society will shift from extractive to regenerative economies. The cases presented here show that this shift is gathering pace and how it is being undertaken. Regenerative entrepreneurship has the potential to drive the transition toward a global economic tipping point from which regenerative economies will emerge. If that tipping point is not reached and the extractive economies continue to dominate, then the possibility of a resilient and flourishing social-ecological foundation on which stable economies can operate will continue to be threatened.

References

Brolin, J., & Kander, A. (2022). Global trade in the Anthropocene: A review of trends and direction of environmental factor flows during the Great Acceleration. *The Anthropocene Review*, 9(1), 71–110.

Brovkin, V., Brook, E., Williams, J. W., Bathiany, S., Lenton, T. M., Barton, M., ... Yu, Z. (2021). Past abrupt changes, tipping points and cascading impacts in the Earth system. *Nature Geoscience*, 14(8), 550–558. doi:10.1038/s41561-021-00790-5

Edwards, M., Benn, S., & Starik, M. (2017). Business cases for sustainability-integrated management education. In J. A. Arevalo & S. F. Mitchell (Eds.), *Handbook of Sustainability in Management Education* (pp. 45–66). New York, NY: Edward Elgar Publishing.

Friedman, M. (1970). The social responsibility of business is to increase its profits. *New York Times Magazine*, pp. 173–178.

Fullerton, J. (2015). *Regenerative Capitalism*. Greenwich, CT: Capital Institute.

Gentile, M. C. (2010). *Giving Voice to Values: How to Speak Your Mind When You Know What's Right*. New Haven, CT: Yale University Press.

Gentile, M. C. (2016). Listening for Values. *Humanist Management Journal*, 1, 107–111.

Hirschman, A. O. (1970). *Exit, Voice, and Loyalty: Responses to Decline in Firms, Organizations, and States*. Cambridge, MA: Harvard University Press.

Hutchins, G., & Storm, L. (2019). *Regenerative Leadership: The DNA of Life-Affirming 21st Century Organizations*. Kent, UK: eBook Partnership.

Kunkel, S., & Tyfield, D. (2021). Digitalisation, sustainable industrialisation and digital rebound – Asking the right questions for a strategic research agenda. *Energy Research & Social Science*, 82, 102295. doi:10.1016/j.erss.2021.102295

Landrum, N. E. (2018). Stages of corporate sustainability: Integrating the strong sustainability worldview. *Organization & Environment*, 31(4), 287–313.

Mazzucato, M. (2013). Financing innovation: Creative destruction vs. destructive creation. *Industrial and Corporate Change*, 22(4), 851–867.

Meadows, D. (2009). Leverage points: Places to intervene in a system. *Solutions, 1*(1), 41–49.

Raworth, K. (2012). A safe and just space for humanity: Can we live within the doughnut. *Oxfam Policy and Practice: Climate Change and Resilience, 8*(1), 1–26.

Raworth, K. (2020). *Business Meets the Doughnut*. Retrieved from https://doughnuteconomics.org

Rindova, V., Barry, D., & Ketchen, J. D. J. (2009). Entrepreneuring as emancipation. *Academy of Management Review, 34*(3), 477–491.

Rockström, J., & Gaffney, O. (2021). *Breaking Boundaries: The Science of Our Planet*. New York, NY: Random House.

Roser, M. (2021). Extreme poverty: How far have we come, and how far do we still have to go? Retrieved from https://ourworldindata.org/extreme-poverty-in-brief

Sachs, J. D., Schmidt-Traub, G., Mazzucato, M., Messner, D., Nakicenovic, N., & Rockström, J. (2019). Six transformations to achieve the sustainable development goals. *Nature Sustainability, 2*(9), 805–814. doi:10.1038/s41893-019-0352-9

Soete, L. (2013). Is innovation always good. In J. Fagerberg, B. Martin, & E. Andersen (Eds.), *Innovation Studies: Evolution and Future Challenges* (pp. 134–144).

Steffen, W., Broadgate, W., Deutsch, L., Gaffney, O., & Ludwig, C. (2015). The trajectory of the Anthropocene: The great acceleration. *The Anthropocene Review, 2*(1), 81–98.

Sternad, D., Kennelly, J. J., & Bradley, F. (2016). *Digging Deeper: How Purpose-Driven Enterprises Create Real Value*. Austin, TX: Greenleaf.

Wesselink, R., Blok, V., van Leur, S., Lans, T., & Dentoni, D. (2015). Individual competencies for managers engaged in corporate sustainable management practices. *Journal of Cleaner Production, 106*, 497–506. doi:10.1016/j.jclepro.2014.10.093

Wiedmann, T., Lenzen, M., Keyßer, L. T., & Steinberger, J. K. (2020). Scientists' warning on affluence. *Nature Communications, 11*(1), 3107.

GLOSSARY

4 Returns framework   Commonland's investment model of economic, social, environmental, and inspirational returns.

7 Giving Voice to Values (GVV) Pillars   The 7 core features of GVV that together form the action plan for addressing ethical challenges and opportunities.

12 GVV Assumptions   The 12 propositions that form the foundation for the GVV pedagogy, for example that voicing one's concerns strengthens the capacity to do it again.

Anthropocene   The global epoch where human activities have become the major force in the biophysical and geological changes on the planet.

Biogeochemical flows   One of the nine fundamental planetary processes that mostly involves the production and flow of fertilizing nutrients such as nitrogen and phosphorus.

Biomass   The weight of living material.

Biosphere integrity   One of the nine fundamental planetary processes, which includes flora, fauna, and the diversity of terrestrial and marine-based living systems and their habitats.

Business-As-Usual (BAU)   Profit-driven, market-based economic activity that sees sustainability primarily as a government issue of regulation and consumer choice.

Business-to-business (B2B)   Businesses that deal solely with other businesses in buying and selling goods and services.

Choice   The GVV pillar proposing that people always have the choice to voice their values.

Circularity   The key principle of the circular economy that aims for zero waste from industrial activity. It can be applied at multiple levels, from product and firm-level to regional industry, national, and international levels.

Circular economy   An economy based on principles such as "closing the loop", reducing the flow and prolonging the life of goods.

Climate change   Global changes in the climate due to increasing levels of greenhouse gasses trapping energy within the Earth system. One of the core "Planetary Boundaries".

CO_2   Carbon dioxide, the main greenhouse gas (GHG).

CO_2 equivalents (CO_2e)   Chemical compounds other than CO_2 that cause climate change, for example, methane and nitrous oxide.

Collaborative advantage   The advantages that business benefit from when they collaborate with other businesses and stakeholders.

Conventional business world   The global system of trade and commerce that drives Business-As-Usual operations.

Culture gaps   Misalignments between the values of the members and the organization.

Developmental entrenchment   The continuation of a developmental characteristic that becomes maladaptive at a later stage of development.

Equality   Fairness based on individual differences.

Espoused values   Those values that organizations aim to better embody in the future.

Ethical dilemma   A values-based choice that someone finds confronting or challenging.

Ethical opportunity   A values-based opportunity from which a social benefit could be created.

Ethical behavior   Actions that have moral value.

Eutrophication   The rapid degradation of water-based ecosystems through excessive nutrient loads and subsequent algal blooms.

Expectation gaps   Misalignments between who the person is now and who they intend to be in the future.

False dichotomy   The framing of an ethical challenge in terms of only two possible choices.

Freshwater use   One of the nine fundamental planetary processes that includes all freshwater systems. It includes blue water, that is, all the freshwater in rivers, streams and lakes and green freshwater, that is, all the water and moisture in soil and aquafer systems.

Giving Voice to Values (GVV)   An action-based pedagogy and theory of business ethics that supports personal voice, competency development, and innovation for addressing ethical challenges and opportunities.

Greenhouse gas (GHG)   A gas (carbon dioxide, methane, etc.) that causes the atmospheric greenhouse effect; that is, atmospheric warming and insulation of the Earth system.

Greenwashing   A form of corporate marketing or public relations that presents a façade of environmental concern, action, and product development when none exists.

Gross Domestic Product (GDP)   GDP is the total market monetary value of all the final goods and services produced and sold in a specific period by a country or group of countries.

Intergenerational   A timeframe that goes across multiple human generations (typically 25 years per generation).

Intrapreneurship   The internal process of an organization creating new value within its own operations. An intrapreneur is an individual who initiates that internal value creation.

Land system change   One of the nine fundamental planetary processes that involves both the changing patterns of human use of land, for example, urbanization and agricultural practices, and the impacts of that use, for example, desertification and habitat loss.

Leadership gaps   Misalignments between current values and those espoused by the organization.

Moral action   Doing or saying something in the context of a moral challenge or opportunity.

Moral awareness   Consciousness of the moral dimension of both internal, psychological, and external social environments.

Moral decision-making   An ethical judgment.

Moral imagination   Creative thinking applied to ethics.

Moral intent   Deliberate and ethically motivated action.

Moral silence/muteness   Not acting on, or speaking up about, recognized ethical challenges or opportunities.

Moral myopia/blindness   The inability to see an ethical issue or its implications clearly or at all.

Net positive   Regenerating the life-giving and life-supporting potential of a system.

NGO   Non-Government Organization

Normalization   The GVV pillar proposing that ethical challenges and opportunities are normal, frequent, everyday events.

Ocean acidification   One of the nine fundamental planetary processes that focuses on the state of health of the oceans as measured in its level of acidity.

Personal values   Those values which individuals currently hold.

Planetary boundaries   Planetary boundaries are empirically measurable limits for the nine planetary processes that create global biophysical stability. There are two basic boundaries: those that define safe zones from zones of increasing risk and those that demarcate increasing risk from high-risk zones of unpredictable state shifts.

Prosocial behavior   Acts that are intentionally intended to benefit others.

Purpose   The GVV pillar proposing that broadly defining personal and professional purpose aids in developing capacities for voicing values.

Rationalizations   The GVV pillar proposing values can be silenced by inhibiting reasons called rationalizations, of which there are several common categories

Regenerative agriculture   A restoration and renewal approach to food and farming systems that prioritizes the integrity and resilience of natural systems so that economic and social benefits are integrated within an ecological context.

Regenerative farming   The local form of regenerative agriculture.

Regenerative business   Business that aims for positive intergenerational contributions to social-ecological resilience and economic prosperity through the creation of real value for all stakeholders and rightholders via participatory empowerment and technology and nature-based solutions.

Regenerative capitalism   A regenerative and market-based economic system based on multiple forms of capital, e.g., social, natural, economic, culture, intellectual, and technological capital.

Regenerative economy   An economy that is based on regenerative business and government regulations that support regenerativity.

Regenerative entrepreneur   A person who uses financial resources to create social-ecological value over the long term.

Regenerative organization   An organized group committed to restoring and rebuilding social-ecological resilience and well-being.

Resilience   The stabilizing, adaptive, and transformative capacities of a social-ecological system.

Rightholders   A person or entity that holds a right of ownership, decision-making power, moral recognition or consultation.

Self-knowledge and alignment   The GVV pillar proposing that individuals can develop their ethical competencies through using self-knowledge, reflecting on self-stories, and analyzing mis/alignments between personal and collective values.

Shared values   Those values that organizations currently hold.

Social-ecological system   The interdependent and co-creative nature of all social and ecological systems.

Stakeholders   People, human communities, and biophysical systems who have interests in, or are impacted by, the operations of a business or organization.

Status quo   The current system of organizing and social practice.

Sustainability, sustainable development   Social systems and economic development provide for the needs of the current population without compromising the ability of future populations to meet their own needs.

Safe and just operating space   The planetary state that provides for human flourishing and the regeneration of resilient and diverse biophysical and ecological systems. Defined as the zone between a sufficient social foundation to provide universal social equities while not exceeding the environmental limits of the biophysical systems of the planet.

Systems thinking   Reasoning that generates multiple options and systemic solutions without reduction to false dichotomies or simplistic dualities.

Values   The GVV pillar proposing that individuals and organizations have a small number of core beliefs that guide them toward their goals and visions of the future.

Vision gaps   Misalignments between the future goals and purposes of organizational members and the formal organization.

Voice   The GVV pillar proposing that practicing expressing values helps to build ethical competencies over time.

Well-being   The individual and collective experience of health, happiness, prosperity, inclusion, and control over important aspects of personal and community life.

INDEX

Pages in *italics* refer to figures.

4 Returns Framework 85–86, 92–93, 97–101, 105, 110–111, 186, 193
7 Pillars 27, 34–50; choice 36–37, 48–49, 53–84, 194; normalization 37–39, 48, 85–111, 196; purpose 3, 13, 18–21, 28–31, 39–40, 48–49, 54, 86, 114, 117–118, 130–135, 156, 172, 196; rationalization 3, 21, 46–50, 149–168, 196; self-story 3, 21, 41, 43, 49–50, 112–138, *132*; voice 87, 101, 139–150, 153–154, 156–168
12 Assumptions 27, 32–34, 176

Altiplano Estepario 93–94, 110
Anthropocene 5–9, 70, 170, 183

Backcasting 78–79
Big Disconnect 11
Biodiversity 5, 8, 10, 13, 16, 23–24, 31, 55, 74, 86, 94, 96, 129, 141, 147, 154, 170, 182, 190; functional 23; genetic 23

Biophysical systems 6, 10, 66, 72, 87, 137, 170, 197; atmosphere 5, 9, 14; biosphere 10, 12–13, 17, 30, 59, 70, 88, 102, 141, 185, 189, 193
Business ethics 3, 8, 20–21, 27–52, 76, 167, 171, 187–188, 195
Business within planetary boundaries 13, 17, 141
Business, society, and nature nexus 20, 56, 90, 144
Business-As-Usual (BAU) 7–8, 12, 87, 95, 155, 157–158, 160, 174–175, 181, 187–190, 193

Carbon sequestration 140, 142, 147
Carrying capacity 17, 65–66
Churchill, Winston 2
Circular economy 32, 57, 117, 120, 123, 130, 132, 178, 194
Climate Change 2–3, 5, 7, 9, 14, 31, 55, 64, 66–67, 72, 74, 93, 121, 129, 141, 170, 182, 184, 190, 194

Co-evolutionary 101
Collaboration 104, 109, 113, 118, 154, 172, 180, 186
Collapse awareness 14, 31, 49, 53, 55, 58–63, 65–66, 68, 77, 170
Commonland **19**–20, 49, 85–111, 189
Compartmentalization 44, 151
Competition 8, 92, 104, 143
Complexity thinking 12, 22, 30, 42, 55, 173
Cooperation 57, 122
Covid-19 6–7, 9, 58
Custodian 63, 70–71, 77; see also Stewardship

Decarbonization 3, 141–142
Developmental entrenchment 53, 71–73, 75, 78
Doughnut economics 16–18, 56, 174
Drawdown 9

Earth Overshoot Day 9–10, 170
Earth Regenerators **19**–20, 49, 53–83, 180
Earth system science 1, 5, 11, 13, 16, 37, 60, 71
Economic growth 6, 11, 14, 39, 46–47, 72, 145, 158, 183, 187, 189
Embedded view 12, 173, 182
Empowerment 12, 21, 32, 35, 47, 109, 115, 117, 130, 160, 176
Entrepreneurship creative destruction 174–175; destructive creation 174–175; emancipation 117, 132, 178; regenerative 3, 16, 21, 48, 53, 55–56, 58, 63, 73, 85, 87, 95–101, 105, 130, 139–140, 158, 166, 171–183, 185–186, 190, 197; sustainable 197
Ethical opportunity 1, 18, 39, 101, 128–129, 159–160, 171, 186

Ethics 33, 74; descriptive 33, 74; normative 11, 27, 29, 37, 41, 74, 154, 185; pedagogy 3, 28–29, 34, 46, 49, 193; performative 4, 32–34, 36, 48–49, 52, 74

False dichotomies 47, 99–100, 158–159, 197
Foresight 38
Fossil fuels 2, 5
Freedom 34, 55, 95, 99, 130
Friedman, Milton 184

Gaffney, Owen 5, 170, 182
Gentile, Mary 3, 27–29, 32, 35–36, 40–41, 45, 48, 50, 76, 136–137, 163, 167, 175–176, 184
GHG emissions 8–10, 25, 126–127, 142
Giving Voice to Values 3–4, 18, 20, 22, 27–29, 32–34, 36, 39–41, 43, 50, 56, 101, 157, 167, 186–189, 193–198
Great Acceleration 6, 182
Greenwash 99, 104, 118, 154, 195
Guterres, António 3, 7

Hirschman, Albert 50, 184
Holocene 6
Human boundaries metaphor 15
Human Rights 82, 113, 116, 118, 125, 185
Humanium Metal **19**, 21, 32, 40, 49, 112–138, 178

Imagination 12, 28, 37, 75, 105, 109, 160, 179, 195
Indigenous 8, 13, 61, 102, 182
Individuell Människohjälp (IM) **19**, 21, 112–113
Inner Development Goals 41–42, 178–179

Inspirational returns 8, **19**, 86–102, 105–106

Integrity 7, 13, 35, 42–44, 64, 67, 93, 117, 119, 141, 143, 148, 160, 172, 180–181, 193

Interdependency 12, 35, 109, 173

Intergenerational 13, 35, 65, 73, 96, 109, 146, 177–178, 181–182, 195–196

Intergovernmental Panel on Climate Change (IPCC) 3, 7, 9

Landrum, Nancy 101, 181, 190

Mission Zero 9–10, 170, 194

Moral behavior 10, 21, 28–29, 36, 38–41, 48, 64, 74, 117, 150, 183–188, 195

Moral imagination 4, 28, 32, 195

Moral muteness 32, 50–51, 81, 196

Moral silence 21, 32–33, 38, 46–47, 117, 129, 176–177, 181, 187, 189, 196

Nature-based solutions 13, 144, 177, 196

Paradox of choice 53, 75, 77

Planetary Boundaries 13, 15, 17, 63, 66, 141, 194, 196; biodiversity 5, 8, 10, 13, 16, 23–24, 31, 55, 74, 86, 94, 96, 129, 141, 147, 154, 170, 182; climate change 14, 22–25, 27, 29, 31, 55, 64, 66–67, 72, 74, 93, 121, 129, 141, 170, 184, 190, 194; fresh water 8, 10, 13, 16, 58, 70, 86, 90, 94, 96, 141, 182, 194; geochemical flows 5, 13, 16, 141, 193–194; land system change 5, 8, 13, 16, 20, 49, 71, 73–74, 85–111, 181–184, 190, 195; novel entities 5, 8, 13, 16, 74; ocean acidification 5, 8, 10, 13–14, 58, 70, 141, 147, 196

Planetary processes 3, 15, 66, 170, 173, 193, 195–196

Pollution 6, 8, 10, 55, 57, 74, 177, 182, 196

Profit 8, 18, 38, 40, 46–48, 56, 91, 103–104, 115, 124, 132, 142–143, 145, 148–149, 155, 158, 172–175, 177, 180–181, 183–184

Prosocial 59, 62, 66–69, 74, 76–77, 81, 196

Rationalization process 3, 21, 46–49, 99, 149–151, 164–165, 173, 176–177, 196

Real value 9, 12, 25, 49, 89, 117, 155, 174–175, 182

Regenerative 1–26 *see* regenerativity; business 1, 3, 10–11, 18, 20–21, 27, 37, 40, 48, 55–57, 82, 86, 95, 105–106, 109, 140, 155–161, 167, 169–170, 172–174, 178, 185–186, 189–190, 196–197; economics 59, 86, 174, 181; leadership 64–65, 124, 129, 131, 143, 160, 181–182; sustainability 1, 35, 44, 49–50, 59, 61, 63, 93, 95–96, 113, 129, 133, 139, 169–171, 174, 177, 181, 185, 189–190

Regenerativity 1–26 *see* regenerative; agriculture 82, 94, 110, 140, 142, 182; education 54, 59, 61, 71, 73–75, 90, 92, 100, 130, 171, 179, 182; investment 35, 44, 47, 49, 72, 82, 91–93, 98–102, 115, 118–119, 150–156, 190, 193; organizations 2, 10, 13, 20, 34, 49, 53, 74, 87, 139–140, 157, 169, 171–173, 177–178, 181, 190, 194

Relationality 41, 177–181

Resilience 6, 8, 10–11, 13, 15, 55, 66, 70, 92, 96, 106, 117, 130, 170, 174–175, 180, 183, 190, 196

Responsibility 8, 21, 29, 32, 35, 42, 46, 49, 53, 57, 64–65, 70–71, 77, 133, 144–145, 148, 151, 167, 182–184, 190
Rightholder 12, 65, 82, 127–128, 196–197
Rockström, Johan 5, 9, 14, 15

Safe and just operating space 17, 102, 170, 174, 197
Safe operating space 9, 14, 15, 17
Scale of impact 9–12, 14, 55, 58–62, 66, 85–86, 95–96, 100, 128, 142, 147, 170, 173
Sixth Mass Extinction 5, **19**, 66
Social inequality 16, 183
Social sustainability 17, 30, 31, 127, 129, 131, 181
Social-ecological system 10, 12, 20, 35, 42, 71, 87, 91–92, 103, 121, 137, 142, 149, 155–159, 172, 175, 197
Spaceship Earth 3
Spirituality 97
Stakeholder 12, 20, 22, 28, 39, 46, 57, 65, 87, 89–97, 99–100, 102, 104, 109, 119–122, 124, 126–129, 131, 140, 142, 146–155, 159–160, 165, 172, 176–179, 183, 194, 196–197
Steffen, Will 5–6, 15, 66, 182
Stewardship 70–71, 140–141, 148–149, 174
Sustainability 169–192; competencies 11–12, 22, 29–31, 41, 45, 48, 130, 173, 185, 197; design 13, 18, 53–56, 58–59, 61, 64–65, 67–75, 77, 81, 86, 113–115, 118, 127, 146, 149, 164; innovation 17, 72, 173–174, 176, 182
Sustainability-as-flourishing 10–12, 55, 87, 95, 102, 172–173, 176, 182
Sweet spot of societal change 179, 180
Systems thinking 12, 22, 30, 173, 185, 197

Technology 13, 30, 62, 109, 140, 144, 177, 182, 196
The Seaweed Company **19**, 21, 49, 139–168, 176–177, 189
Three pillars of sustainability 129–130
Tipping point 5, 7, 14, 16, 66, 74, 82–83, 102, 110, 129, 170, 172, 190; social tipping point 102, 172

United Nations 2, 7–8, 41, 114, 128, 184

Values gaps 43–44, 180, 194–195, 198
Vicious cycle 115, 176
Virtuous cycle 121, 176–177
Vision 21, 29, 39–40, 43–44, 74, 91–92, 94, 98, 109, 117, 145, 175, 178, 198

Well-being 12, 67, 69–70, 96, 125, 130, 145–146, 170, 174, 183, 197

Zoonotic spillover 7

Printed in the United States
by Baker & Taylor Publisher Services